GREG HOLSCLAW

Supernatural Theology

Discovering Your Spiritual Gifts

First published by Revival Valley Media 2019

Unless otherwise noted, all Bible references are from the ESV translation. Bible references are within the limitations that the ESV allows for inclusion in books and articles.

At times, some personal identifiable details have been changed to protect the privacy of individuals whose life stories are described.

In the digital formats of this book, some links to books or references may include Amazon.com affiliate information in the links.

SELECTED ENDORSEMENTS (full endorsements before the Introduction)

"We are in a season where healthy theology in the charismatic movement is vital, and where the expression of the gifts of the Spirit has never been more necessary for the extension of the Kingdom of God. Greg's solid work in "Supernatural Theology" creates a pathway to that healthy theology ... He has tackled complex concepts in his book "Supernatural Theology" and has made them relatable to our every day lives."
~ Rev. Landen Dorsch, Lead Pastor Gateway Family Church (Alberta, Canada), Author of Renovated for Glory, Host of Kingdom Wild

"God is moving in the supernatural all over the world. It's time to discover what the Bible actually reveals about it all, and allow our theology to be adjusted and expanded by the heart of God and His truth. We are in a Kairos moment in history. Greg's book, Supernatural Theology, bids us enter in."
~ Dr Kim Maas, Doctorate in Ministry, Founder Kim Maas Ministries, Author & International Speaker, https://kimmaas.com

"In his book, Supernatural Theology, Greg brilliantly communicates our heavenly Father's invitation and plan for us to encounter Him by means of His own Spirit and through the spiritual gifts given to us that express His nature. Greg provides a necessary bridge between those who would emphasize the power of the Spirit and those who would emphasize the truth of God's word to be able to honor, appreciate and even embrace what the other holds so dear."
~ Brent Lokker, Lead Pastor, Author of Always Loved: You are God's Treasure, Not His Project

"Greg Holsclaw, is a student of Scripture and a practitioner of Spiritual gifts ... this book will give you greater understanding of the theological underpinnings that you need to know in order to lead a diverse workplace to a place of unity and respect regarding the use of the gifts in your conference room prayer gatherings, lunch time Bible studies, and worship gatherings in the workplace ... you will come to appreciate an approach that leads you into the word of truth AND the power of the Spirit!"
~ Roy Tinklenberg, Founder Faith and Work Movement Global, Catalyzing 100s of Workplace Fellowships, Masters in Divinity, https://www.faithandworkmovement.org

First edition

ISBN: 978-0-9963745-1-4

This book was professionally typeset on Reedsy.
Find out more at reedsy.com

To Tracy, my wife, and to my mom and dad.
You have all made innumerable deposits in my life.

Contents

Acknowledgement

Without my wonderful wife, Tracy, I would have never finished. Through your constant encouragements and generosity in creating space and time for me to write, you were an amazing support throughout the multi-year journey to compose, edit and finish this project.

A special thanks to James Stoner Holk for your high level feedback, an sharpening of iron on iron effort, and to Dorothy Mitchell for helping polish this manuscript.

Also, I want to thank the Stirring Church, the Lift Community and Revival Valley for allowing me to test these ideas, sharpen the text, and for giving me space to write.

ENDORSEMENTS

"We are in a season where healthy theology in the charismatic movement is vital, and where the expression of the Gifts of the Spirit has never been more necessary for the extension of the Kingdom of God. Greg's solid work in "Supernatural Theology" creates a pathway to that healthy theology. It is said that smart people celebrate complex concepts, but brilliant people take complex concepts and make them simple. Greg Holsclaw is one of the brilliant ones. He has tackled complex concepts in his book "Supernatural Theology" and has made them relatable to our every day lives."

~ Rev. Landen Dorsch, Lead Pastor Gateway Family Church (Alberta, Canada), Author of Renovated for Glory, Host of Kingdom Wild

"Like so many of us, there was a time when Greg Holsclaw had "a theology that allowed for God to move like this on an infrequent basis but no expectant belief He delighted in doing such things." Also like so many of us, he found out there is so much more. God is moving in the supernatural all over the world. It's time to discover what the Bible actually reveals about it all, and allow our theology to be adjusted and expanded by the heart of God and His truth. Greg Holsclaw helps us do just that. We are in a Kairos moment in history. Greg's book, Supernatural Theology, bids us enter in."

~ Dr Kim Maas, Doctorate in Ministry, Founder Kim Maas Ministries, Author & International Speaker, https://kim-maas.com

"In his book, Supernatural Theology, Greg brilliantly communicates our heavenly Father's invitation and plan for us to encounter Him by means of His own Spirit and through the spiritual gifts given to us that express His nature. Greg provides a necessary bridge between those who would emphasize the power of the Spirit and those who would emphasize the truth of God's word to be able to honor, appreciate and even embrace what the other holds so dear. This practical book will inspire you and instruct you on how to live in the supernatural realm of God's Kingdom as a regular way of life. Through Greg's writings, you will see the imprint of an author who deeply loves

God, who loves His Word, and who loves the freedom and power of God's Spirit. Enjoy the journey into the truth and mystery of the heart of God!"

~ Brent Lokker, Lead Pastor, Author of Always Loved: You are God's Treasure, Not His Project

"When leaders of workplace fellowships gather Christians together in the Silicon Valley or other corporate settings, group members come together from vast varieties of church backgrounds. One area of difference that often surfaces in theologically eclectic environments is an individual's belief about engaging the gifts of the Holy Spirit. Greg Holsclaw, is a Silicon Valley engineer, a student of scripture and a practitioner of Spiritual gifts. While his book may not specifically show you how to create policies that will navigate the complexity of leading a workplace fellowship, it will give you greater understanding of the theological underpinnings that you need to know in order to lead a diverse workplace to a place of unity and respect regarding the use of spiritual gifts in your conference room prayer gatherings, lunch time Bible studies, and worship gatherings in the workplace. You will come to appreciate an approach that leads you into the word of truth AND the power of the Spirit!"

~ Roy Tinklenberg, Founder Faith and Work Movement Global, Catalyzing 100s of Workplace Fellowships, Masters in Divinity, https://www.faithandworkmovement.org

"Spiritual gifts have often been a dividing line for many Christian denominations. In Greg Holsclaw's new book the theology of the gifts of the Holy Spirit is clearly laid out. Greg offers practical understanding and an invitation for every believer in

Christ to step forward with the mandate of scripture to do the greater things that Jesus said we would do. This book is a must read and your invitation to live the supernatural life you are destined to live!"

~ Reverend Joanne Moody, Founder Agape Freedom Fighters, Author & International Speaker, https://www.agapefreedomfighters.org

"Greg Holsclaw's book Supernatural Theology introduces the reader to the gifts of the Holy Spirit with his experiential knowledge and wisdom. He builds a foundation from his theological background and adds practical steps to go deeper into an experience with each of the spiritual gifts. He adds nuances to traditional understanding and bridges the gap between talking about the gifts and describing real life experiences. He unpacks the links between the love of God and the power of God, between faith and healing, and between the gift of prophecy and the modern day prophetic word. He demonstrates how the gifts can be developed through practice with exercises. This book is an essential resource for theological discussions as well as practical ways to operate in the supernatural gifts of the Holy Spirit.

~ Stephanie Shoquist, MA Theology, Director Silicon Valley Healing Rooms, Founder of Hearts Aligned Ministries

INTRODUCTION

It was a Saturday evening, a group of us were spending time at a friend's house (who later would become my wife), playing on the three quarter size pool table, eating chips and popcorn. We were all from the college group at the church I had attended since early high school. Sometimes we talked about theology, sometimes we challenged each other regarding what Jesus would do in certain situations, and other times, like this night, we were young adults hanging out without a care in the world simply playing games.

A friend walked in late; she had just received a message from another girl in the college group. Her dad was in the hospital rapidly dying of an unknown disease that was causing all of his organs to fail. He was not expected to make it through the night, and definitely not the weekend.

We paused hanging out and gathered around to pray for a bit. A short prayer started bubbling up in my heart, and with some urgency I prayed something like this: "Lord, we pray that Mr. Smith (not his real name) would be healed. That he would be healed and discharged from the hospital before the end of tomorrow evening. In your name Jesus, amen."

And that is exactly what happened! Three days later at the regular Tuesday night college group meeting, we received a report about the young lady's father. He had made a dramatic turnaround, and was discharged the next evening after we prayed. He had gone from the edge of death to good health and out of the hospital in under 24 hours!

I wish I could report that this was a transformational moment for my friends and me. It would have been great if this experience led to a heightened pursuit of God, of what He was doing, and of what He wanted to do among us. I wish that this was the start of some great adventure into the love and power that God wanted to regularly display though His people to draw the world to Himself. Sadly, none of these things happened.

Instead, we praised God for a moment. We marveled at the miracle God did in our midst, then packaged up the memory and moved on with our lives. The ripples of this life-and-death miraculous healing had no lasting effect on us at all. We had no fertile soil for this experience to take root in, no regular testimony to water and magnify what God had done in our midst, and no expectation that He might do it again.

We had a theology that allowed for God to move like this on an infrequent basis but no expectant belief that He delighted in doing such things. This miracle became a memory of an event, a fact marked down in history, almost treated like the exception that proves the rule. My theology was incomplete; it did not lead me to expect much from God. My beliefs never left the pages of the Bible. The ways of God I read about in the Book of Acts and the way Paul described the church in his Epistles seemed distant to me. I believed God could heal on occasion or might even give a missionary the ability to rapidly learn a new language. But I also believed that he most likely would not do that in my life, in my surroundings, and He most definitely would not do it on a regular basis.

At the time of this healing I had read through the Bible at least once and was working through it a second time. All the churches I attended were Bible-believing evangelical churches with seminary-trained pastors with deep, rich Bible studies. We believed God had the ability to do the miraculous, to speak to His people, and to touch them, but He just did not do it very often. Only the select or those in very special need would be visited by God in such ways, like the young lady's father.

Over the next 12 years, I would get married, finish college, lead small groups at various churches, and even coach small group leaders. My wife and I raised up new leaders, cared for people, and stirred many to faith and godliness in Jesus. I had many spiritual warfare encounters, went on missions trips abroad, heard from God on 'the big' topics, tried to be faithful in all God asked of me, and I saw my wife healed by the hand of God. But my theology and experience was generally unchanged.

But then something shifted about 10 years ago. I landed in a group of people whose expectations in God were plainly different than mine. They believed God wanted to answer prayer even as we spoke and wanted to use us to do miracles. They believed God would speak each day through His Word, in our hearts, and through others as directed by the Holy Spirit. Their theology and doctrine generally matched mine, but their expectation in God was very different. This excited me, sending me on a new pursuit into the ways of God.

Same Faith, Different Walk

Before meeting this group of people who were passionately pursuing the gifts of the Holy Spirit, my life with God was generally fulfilling, and my belief in Jesus Christ never wavered. I grew in love and appreciation for all He had done for me. I was constantly told I was a rock of faith and had a kind heart.

I was a shepherding type of person, an unwavering soul that others found strength in and I knew God loved me.

My theology had not really grown or changed, but my walk with Christ changed. The doctrines and theologies that built upon the Bible and the evangelical church foundation of my young adulthood were still there, just as solid as when the Lord poured them. What changed were my expectations and practices surrounding my faith in Christ and my pursuit of the Holy Spirit, which resulted in a new kind of everyday Christian life.

My hope in writing this book is to stimulate a similar journey in you. I will start by reaffirming the foundational theology and tenets of Christian faith we all share. But at the same time, I seek to shift your expectations concerning what God will do in and through us in our daily lives, a life that the Bible says should be a continually powerful, spiritually-gifted life.

Many of the verses you may have read many times, but this time I am hoping you see and draw new connections and applications to your daily life. We will look at verses and stories in-depth, highlighting points that at times maybe were too quickly acknowledged but not deeply believed or you have yet to turn into action! This is a book to help you on your journey to expect and want more; God wants more in our lives, and we should want it, too.

How to Read this Book

In many ways, all our theology should turn into action that leads us to love God and love people more in accordance with the great commandments (Matthew 22:36-40) and fulfill the great commission (Matthew 28:18-20). A practical and practiced theology is more useful to ourselves and to the world than an intellectual concept that never spurs us to action. Therefore, throughout this book I will try to give direct ways we can immediately apply our theology to daily life.

In Part 1 of the book, I build a biblical foundation regarding the presence and power of the Holy Spirit in our lives. First, we seek to be worshipers in spirit and in truth (John 4:24) with a greater expectation of the Holy Spirit in our lives. Next we address what the Holy Spirit does in our lives. We will discuss well-known foundational topics like salvation, new birth, and sealing and indwelling of the Holy Spirit in us. Then we will move on to the continuing power of the Holy Spirit to sustain us through persecution and living daily in power. Part 1 ends with a discussion of one of the six foundational truths found in Hebrews 6:1-2 regarding the laying on of hands to explore how we stir up the gifts of God in ourselves and others.

As we participate with the Holy Spirit in us, we must understand the spiritual gifts and the way He wants to see us move. Part 2 of this book will include study, practical examples, and personal application of the various gifts of the Holy Spirit as recorded in 1 Corinthians 12:8-10. These chapters each end with questions and reflections to help us immediately put these truths into action.

We will focus on these spiritual gifts for a few reasons. First, unlike the gifts listed in Romans 12 or Ephesians 4, these gifts are specifically attributed to the Holy Spirit. Second, in my experience, the gifts in Romans 12 are more readily understood, accepted, and honored in most churches and fellowships, while the 1 Corinthian 12 spiritual gifts tend to be pursued less or even left unused. So this book will limit its scope to the 1 Corinthians 12:8-10 gifts. See Appendix B for a full list of spiritual gifts and a concise definition of each.

As we discuss the gifts in Part 2, we will adhere to a consistent format to outline the firm Biblical basis for each spiritual gift. We will also explore how and why we continue to look for God to move in these ways today. A supernatural theology is about moving from merely 'knowing about God' to 'believing He is WITH us.' If He is really with us, then His presence should be present with us each and every day, not just in a spiritual way, but in a supernatural way. Each chapter will follow the same format:

1. Introduce the spiritual gift
2. Show the ways of God from the Old Testament and how they help us understand the Holy Spirit's activity regarding the spiritual gift
3. Show that Jesus taught and lived with Holy Spirit activity in His life and ministry from the Gospel accounts
4. Illustrate that the early Church expected spiritual gifts and spiritual activity to continue in their midst, passed down from each generation of disciples to the next
5. Practical examples and life stories from modern life
6. Discovering Your Gift advice, Faith in Action exercises, and Further Reading suggestions for the pursuit of a particular gift

The path of this book will help inspire you to pursue more of the spiritual gifts available through the Holy Spirit.

Two Sets of Readers

I expect two sets of readers to move through these pages, both benefiting from what will be covered.

First, to the new believers who have recently found their faith in Jesus Christ for salvation: welcome! I urge you not to stop your studies with my book, but to read the Bible in conjunction with it. God will directly show Himself to you through His Word. Do not read it just as history, but be inspired to think that God would, and will, do the same or similar things in your life. Know that many people before you have struggled to actually live out the truths found in the Bible. You are not alone. Be encouraged that you are learning early in your Christian life how to pursue all that God intends you to live.

Second, there are many readers who, like me, are a part of the Bible evangelical tradition (be it baptist, reformed, evangelical non-denominational, anabaptist or another theological stream). You have read your Bible and feel there is a difference between what you read and what you experience. You feel there is more in store for you as you pursue your faith in the Father, the Son and the Holy Spirit, but you are not sure how to move forward. This book is specifically written for you. It took me over 20 years with our Lord to start actually pursuing all that God wanted for me. It is never too late.

Sometimes you may discover a spiritual attribute in your life like wisdom, discernment, prophecy, or healing that outstrips your spiritual maturity. That is because it is a spiritual gift, not something you learned, trained or pursued through study or earned through maturity, spiritual discipline, and a clean Christian lifestyle. The gift may feel bigger than you or beyond what you know how to handle, like a child using a fire hose. Yet the Spirit of God bestowed you with this gift for the betterment of His church. Now you must pursue a deeper relationship with Him to learn how to use the gift wisely and not cause harm. Your love has to grow to catch up with the gifting, and you need maturity and discipline to be able to carry this spiritual gift. This book is for you!

This book is *not* being written to prove that the Holy Spirit is active in the life of the believer today or that the spiritual gifts are all still in operation in the church. The issues with cessationist views are well covered in other books and texts. This book will assume that the Holy Spirit and spiritual gifts are for today, but many of us do not fully understand the spiritual gifts and how to recognize when they are being used.

For both readers, be blessed in the knowledge that God draws near to those who draw near to Him (James 4:8). As I speak of my pursuit of God, and as we study His word, I believe your relationship with God will be strengthened and your faith in Him will increase. Let us pursue Him together in the rich spiritual journey He desires for each of us.

I

FOUNDATIONS IN THE SPIRIT

1

SPIRIT AND TRUTH

"THERE HAS BEEN A SILENT DIVORCE IN THE CHURCH, SPEAKING generally, between the Word and the Spirit. ... But if these two would come together, the simultaneous combination would mean spontaneous combustion."
—R.T. Kendall, *Holy Fire: A Balanced, Biblical Look at the Holy Spirit's Work in Our Lives*

When I was a young man, I attended a church with nearly a thousand people. I earnestly studied church structures by reading books, studying the book of Acts, investigating church boards and committees and even joining in as a student leader on a pastoral search committee. I was an empowered college student leader who loved reading my Bible. I noticed that in the book of Acts, the people hosted large meetings and small house gatherings regularly. They met in the temple to hear the apostles teach and in houses to share meals and fellowship. This seemed very standard and common in the life of the early church.

Then I read *Redefining Revival* by William Beckham. He called this concept the 'two-winged' church. Beckham noted that a church with a 'small group vision' that is never implemented is like a bird who is not using both wings. A bird without one wing cannot fly. Likewise, a bird with two wings that consistently flaps only one of them will not soar or even get off the ground. Such a bird looks capable, but without using both wings, it is grounded. Only when both wings are fully engaged can the bird fly high in the sky.

Beckham's point was that churches needed to focus on both wings of small and large church gatherings. There can be too much either/or thinking in the church and we need to rediscover a set of 'both/and' thinking regarding various topics. Likewise, I believe there is another set of wings most fellowships and gatherings do not make full use of, the wings of worshiping in 'spirit' and in 'truth.'

> *"But the hour is coming, and is now here, when the true worshipers will worship the Father in spirit and truth, for the Father is seeking such people to worship him. God is spirit, and those who worship him must worship in spirit and truth." John 4:23-24*

Being true worshipers in both spirit and truth fulfills the desire of the Father.

Jesus reminds us that we also have to be doers of the word, not just hearers (Matthew 7:24). Words without action is not enough. A practiced vision is needed, not a list of bullet points on paper. A bird that has both wings but only makes use of one of them cannot fly. Both spirit and truth are needed for true worshipers to soar.

Likewise, doctrinal statements affirming the activity of the Holy Spirit, spiritual gifts and the power of God, without any pursuit of them is incomplete. When fellowships do not create space for both pursuits to prosper they are implicitly signaling that both wings are not equally important. If fellowships do not encourage worshiping and serving God through the spirit, or do not encourage regular reading of the Bible, or do not applaud pursuing the things of the Spirit as much they applaud exploring the Truth in Scripture, they are saying one wing is altogether unnecessary.

Unpracticed Doctrine

Dr. Randy Clark relates a prayerful interaction he had with God one day while in his church office. His story illustrates how we can correctly describe a theology of God's Spirit (acknowledging the wing exists) without practicing the things of the Spirit (actually using that wing). An Baptist pastor at the time, he longed to raise up disciples in God's truth. Through his study of the Word, he was convinced that the power and gifts of the Holy Spirit were still available to the churches of Jesus Christ today.

> *First, I was in my office praying, "God, thank You that I'm not a liberal. I believe Jesus did what the Bible says He did. And thank You that I'm not a cessationist. I believe He still does what He did then."*
>
> *I was expecting a "Well done, thou good and faithful servant with whom I am well pleased." But instead I heard from the Lord, "So what?"*
>
> *"What do you mean, so what?" I quickly asked Him. I*

> *heard, "You might as well be a liberal or a cessationist. It isn't enough to say you believe I still do what I did—if you don't know how to move in My gifts, you won't be able to do any more than a liberal or cessationist does."*[1]

He was correct in his doctrine, but God did not approve of his unpracticed system of thought. Fellowships that believed in the gifts of the Spirit but did not practice them were in just as much error as fellowships that believed the spiritual gifts had ceased to operate. Neither group demonstrated the gifts and power of the Holy Spirit.

A pursuit of truth without its practice is a false pursuit. The book of James calls unpracticed faith dead (James 2:14-26). Similarly, things of the Spirit that are preached but not practiced should be considered dead. If you earnestly believed or had faith in those spiritual truths, you would practice them. It is just like that bird with only one wing; it never gets off the ground.

Godly worshiping communities who focus on the truth found in Scripture can layer onto that foundation a practiced theology of being spiritual and Holy Spirit gifted worshipers. The church comes into its fullness when both wings of spirit and truth worship flap fervently in our ascent to God, our Father.

Adding Spirit to Truth

Truth is where I majored in my first decades of walking with the Lord. I knew God's Scriptures, having read the Bible cover to cover many times by the time I was 30. I wrote my

---

1 Randy Clark, *Essential Guide to Healing* (Baker Publishing Group, 2011).

own summaries for every chapter of the Bible and created an expansive personal index of notes. I also truly tried to live according to the plan, principles, and wisdom God revealed through His written word.

Yet I was aware that I did not have a firm handle on the 'spirit' portions of John 4:23-24 and Romans 12:1. Could I worship God correctly in "truth" and still be missing something in the "spirit"? We are all supposed to live a life of sacrifice as spiritual worship, and I did not want to half-worship God. What was I missing pertaining to connecting with God in spirit?

I did not have a grid for 'spiritual things' and had not regularly been exposed to or trained in spiritual worship. I knew God spoke in my prayer times on the really big topics. Things like: who I was to marry, where I should go to college, what I should study. On all other questions and life topics I was told by pastors and leaders that if I washed my heart and mind with Scripture wisdom would follow.

However, the Bible-oriented evangelical churches I grew up in *did* teach the spiritual gifts of teaching, hospitality, giving, evangelism, leadership, and service. Later, when the Holy Spirit did manifest in my life more, I saw the gifts of the Spirit through these new lenses. For example, earlier when I had a good insight for a friend to help them through a problem, I thought I had good natural intuition. Never did I consider the insight was the gift of wisdom (though later I would understand that is how the Holy Spirit flowed through me). I took credit for what the Holy Spirit and I were actually doing together. These spiritual things were a bit of a mystery back then.

Spirit & Truth Worshipers

God has always had a witness in the world to His truth. In the book of Genesis, God walked with Adam and Eve in the garden. Seth, Enoch, Noah, and others knew and worshiped God. God promised Abraham that a people would come from his descendants, a people He would call His own. He always wants to be known by His creation. Not just *felt* spiritually, but actually *known*. Genesis 17:7-8 explains this promise: "I will establish my covenant between me and you and your offspring after you throughout their generations for an everlasting covenant, to be God to you and to your offspring after you... and I will be their God." God was going to make a nation of people who would truly know God and worship Him according to the revelation He was going to give them.

We find the family of Abraham generations later in the book of Exodus. Jacob, his grandson, had moved the family to Egypt. After many generations in Egypt and years of slavery, God worked mighty miracles to free the Israelites and Moses led them toward the promised land. God then gave Moses the laws of the covenant that the nation of Israel were to follow as they live as His people, and worship Him. They were a people of truth with the Law and the Prophets.

When Jesus explained to the Samaritan woman at the well in John 4 that God's worshipers must worship in spirit and truth, He was not broadcasting a change in the script. He was reminding her of what was always true, just as when Moses relayed the commandments of God to the people of Israel in Deuteronomy 6:5, "You shall love the Lord your God with all your heart and with all your soul and with all your might."

The Old Testament emphasizes that God does not only

want dutiful, correctly executed, respectful and truth-filled worship. Hosea 6:6 "For I desire steadfast love and not sacrifice, the knowledge of God rather than burnt offerings." Correct offerings are not the same as knowing and loving God. Proverbs 21:3 reminds us that "to do righteousness and justice is more acceptable to the LORD than sacrifice."

1 Samuel illustrates this point even more forcefully. King Saul had just disobeyed the direction of God. King Saul tried to fall back on Moses' general law of offering spoils of war as a sacrifice instead of obeying the timely word that God had given. 1 Samuel 15:22 records the prophet Samuel's response, "Behold, to obey is better than sacrifice, and to listen than the fat of rams." The relationship with God, loving Him with our hearts, is always above acts of properly conducted worship. God wants our mind, body, and heart filled with expressive love and worship.

Paul pleads in Romans 12:1, "I appeal to you therefore, brothers, by the mercies of God, to present your bodies as a living sacrifice, holy and acceptable to God, which is your spiritual worship." Loving and knowing God, living an upright life and following God's voice is better than physical sacrifices and offerings. God wants the heart and spirit of a person participating in worshiping Him. If our worship stoops to the mere acts and deeds of worship, we are missing the point.

Heart of Worship

God knows we cannot worship this way on our own. If we could be good, righteous worshipers of God all by ourselves, why did Jesus have to come to restore us to God? Through the prophet Ezekiel, God promised that He Himself would help us live righteously and worship Him well.

> *"And I will give you a new heart, and a new spirit I will put within you. And I will remove the heart of stone from your flesh and give you a heart of flesh. And I will put my Spirit within you, and cause you to walk in my statutes and be careful to obey my rules." Ezekiel 36:26-27*

This verse speaks of a time when the Spirit of God lives in people and the Spirit leads them to walk according to God's ways—just like the people Jesus has gathered into His Church and given the Holy Spirit.

> *"... I will put my law within them, and I will write it on their hearts. And I will be their God, and they shall be my people. And no longer shall each one teach his neighbor and each his brother, saying, 'Know the Lord,' for they shall all know me ..." Jeremiah 31:33-34*

Again, God desired to move the nation of Israel (and by faith in Jesus, all people) from an external form of laws and worship into a heart-led form of worship. This Jeremiah verse describes people who are worshipers in spirit with a full understanding of truth. The Spirit of God will show us how to personally and tangibly know God so that we would not need to be taught by one another.

If we are not careful, our worship can turn into just the animations of worship. We place some money in an offering, sing some songs, and give each other encouraging words during the greeting time. The Spirit of God is us helps this not happen.

Mind of Worship

It is good to teach and be taught Scripture. But if our hearts never overflow from a direct connection with the Holy Spirit, then we do not yet 'know the Lord' in the way these Old Testament prophets were speaking of being whole-hearted worshipers. Nor are we doing what Moses directed us—to love God with our whole hearts as well as our souls and our strength.

Turning to the life and ministry of our Lord Jesus is the best way to start establishing what living for God in spirit and truth looks like. Fully God and fully man, Jesus is our example of living with and for God the Father. He did not just teach us how to live; His very life and actions were an example.

Let's look at fasting as a form of worship and a spiritual discipline. Throughout the Old and New Testaments, fasting draws people nearer to God. At Jesus' birth dedication, the prophetess Anna had been in the temple for decades, and "… she never left the temple but worshiped night and day, fasting and praying" (Luke 2:37 ESV). But if fasting leaves the feel of worship and becomes a systematized program of not eating, we can land in the same place the Pharisees ended up. Jesus rebuked them for making a show of fasting.

> *"And when you fast, do not look gloomy like the hypocrites, for they disfigure their faces that their fasting may be seen by others. Truly, I say to you, they have received their reward."* Matthew 6:16

The prophet Isaiah spoke the words of God warning of this. Nearly the whole chapter of Isaiah 58 is focused on the disingenuous fasting the people of Israel had undertaken. God wanted to shift their religious legalistic fasting back to knowing His heart.

> *"Is not this the fast that I choose: to loose the bonds of wickedness, to undo the straps of the yoke, to let the oppressed go free, and to break every yoke? Is it not to share your bread with the hungry and bring the homeless poor into your house; when you see the naked, to cover him, and not to hide yourself from your own flesh?"*
> *Isaiah 58:6-8*

What are we to make of this? Should we pursue righteousness and serve our fellow women and men and not bother with fasting anymore?

One "truth-minded" way of thinking might make a rule that says God does not want us to fast anymore; we should just walk with Him, in righteousness, mercy, and love. Another "truth-minded" person might remind us of the verses where Jesus states that some spiritual oppression is only lifted through prayer and fasting (Matthew 17:21). And what about the verse where Jesus said we should feast when the bridegroom (Jesus) is present, and fast when he is absent (Luke 5:33-35)?

So these two different "truth-minded" believers are at an impasse. Whose truth is superior? Both are true in the sense that God can lead you into both paths at different times in your journey with Him. Sometimes you might be led to fast, other times to feast. Sometimes to prayer, other times to action. As a Spirit-led worshiper, we should not be guided by rules alone, picking one or two favorite verses to pattern our lives around. We should seek the Holy Spirit to guide us in all facets of the truth found in the Bible.

Jesus in Spirit and Truth

In Matthew 4 and Luke 4, Jesus was led by the Holy Spirit to fast for 40 days. This was not a religious fast or a fast directed or encouraged by a man, woman, rule, or custom. He was guided by the Holy Spirit. The result of this fast had a very spiritual effect. He returned to Galilee having overcome the temptations of the devil and filled with the power of the Spirit (Luke 4:14)! The connection with the Father through Jesus' spirit is highlighted when He goes about the work of the Father. John 5:19 says "the Son can do nothing of his own accord, but only what he sees the Father doing. For whatever the Father does, that the Son does likewise." In John 17:8, Jesus prayed, "For I have given them the words that you gave me." Consistently Jesus spoke the words of God and did the Father's work because of His connection to the Father.

Jesus said and did what the Father was saying and doing. This verse does not say that Jesus reflected on what He thought God would do in each circumstance, or considered all the Law and the Prophets and acted accordingly. It says he copied his Father.

God is spirit, John 4:24 reminds us. 1 Corinthians 2:11 states, "For who knows a person's thoughts except the spirit of that person, which is in him? So also no one comprehends the thoughts of God except the Spirit of God." Jesus knew what God was wanting to do because His spirit was connected to the Father.

Nowhere in Scripture does it tell Jesus to go to the pool of Bethesda and heal a lame man (John 5). Nowhere in the Scriptures does it tell Jesus to linger in one place and raise Lazarus from the dead a few days later (John 11). And nowhere in the Scriptures are the compositions of the sermon on the mount (Matt 5-7), or the instructions He gave as He sent out the disciples to preach the kingdom of God (Luke 10). Jesus was not led by Scriptural truth to move, speak and act these ways; He was led by the Spirit of God. In His Spirit, He knew the works the Father was doing. In His Spirit He knew the words the Father was speaking.

But we do not abandon truth for the spirit lead life! Jesus wants us to pursue the 'and' in being worshipers in "spirit and truth" (John 4:24). In John 16:3, Jesus again promises the Holy Spirit, saying He will lead us in all truth. Also Jesus calls the Holy Spirit 'the Spirit of Truth' in John 14:17.

Believers in Spirit & Truth

Studying the truth in Scripture leads to a spiritual connection with God. Connecting with the Spirit of Truth will lead back to God's Word. The spiritual life and the truth-filled life live side by side! If our spirit is being led by the Holy Spirit, then we will be led to truth by the Spirit of Truth. God will lead us into the 'both/and' integration of worship, instead of the 'either/or' mindset that prevails in many church gatherings today.

John 3:6 says "that which is born of the Spirit is spirit." Without the Holy Spirit, given to us when we received Jesus as Lord and Savior, our spirit would still be dead. But being alive now with Christ, our spirit is given life by the Holy Spirit. With the Holy Spirit in us, we can truly worship our God in spirit. This is the promise of a new living heart in Ezekiel 36:26-27 and the law written on our hearts in Jeremiah 31:33-34 fulfilled!

Both/And Thinking

At times, a chasm of either/or thinking has created two great magnetic poles that people and whole churches drift toward in their attitudes of worship. Some people almost exclusively worship God in truth, and others seek to worship God solely in the spiritual sense. Some seek a well-executed musical set, with a well-researched Bible teaching. Others want to establish spontaneous, experiential encounters with the Spirit of God. But God has asked us to worship Him with both aspects together.

The early church was formed with the spirit and truth union intact. My hope is that we could use one such description for the entire church of Christ, that our gatherings would be marked as both spiritual, and truth-filled.

- Spontaneous, connected to God in our spirits
- Orderly, with a systematic expressions of truth
- Joy-filled encounters with God, through the Holy Spirit
- Faith built through careful examination of Scripture

This is how the early churches were established in the book of Acts. In the city of Berea, those who heard Paul's teaching searched the scripture (the Old Testament in their time) to make sure what Paul was saying was true. Acts 17:11 says the Bereans 'received the word with all eagerness, examining the Scriptures daily to see if these things were so.' They were eager truth-seekers and it was commended. Likewise, the Corinthian church was very spiritual, but Paul felt they needed a more instruction regarding spiritual gifts (1 Corinthians 12:1).

Ephesians 1:13 reads, "In him you also, when you heard the

word of truth, the gospel of your salvation, and believed in him, were sealed with the promised Holy Spirit." We receive the word of truth, and then it is sealed with the Spirit of God. Spirit and truth should always be together as we approach God our Father.

Truth-Lead Life

We already read that John 16:13 says that the Holy Spirit will lead us in all truth. But Paul exhorts Timothy and Titus to teach sound doctrine (2 Tim 2:2 & Tit 2:1). Is it the spirit that teaches us, or is it other men and women who teach us? The Bible never accepts this either/or proposition. Never does it say to not listen to men, just listen to the Holy Spirit. Nor is there a command to solely rely on the teaching of leaders. We should be led and taught by the Holy Spirit, as well as led and taught by leaders (as well as encouraged by each other).

Why the both/and structure? I believe it is because none of us perfectly hear from God. Not until heaven will any of us have perfect communion with God, and know His heart fully. Through a mature teacher of the Word or our own study of the Bible, we might find correction (for all Scripture is God-breathed for correction, teaching, training, 2 Timothy 3:16).

At other times, a teacher might lead us astray and we should be open to the Spirit of God leading us back onto the right path. Some of the greatest reformations in the church have occurred when the Spirit of God prompted key leaders to fix wrong theology. From Luther and Calvin to Wesley and Edwards, revivals were sparked when God's truth and God's Spirit were allowed to correctly guide His churches.

Spirit-Lead Life

With the Holy Spirit leading us every day, each day can be different. We see Jesus being led by the Spirit and Father every day for where He should go, what He should do, and even what He should say. When we feel comfortable hearing and receiving personal direction from the Holy Spirit, we can feel confident that we can walk according to the wisdom and revelation given each of us through the Holy Spirit (Ephesians 1:17).

Likewise, the Bible is our daily portion. We receive teaching and sound doctrine from teachers, elders, and leaders among us, just as Titus and Timothy taught the churches Paul sent them to.

"You just read my mail"

As I was continuing my adventures in seeing God move in truth and spirit, I had a friend who was encouraging his father to stop his "old ways" and approach God through the Holy Spirit. My friend's father was an executive pastor of a large church, and my friend was encouraging him to throw off his Biblical, mindful approach to God. At that time I did not know this interaction between father and son had been taking place or the deep internal struggle his father experienced because of it.

This pastor could not wholeheartedly approach God the way his son was encouraging him to. Something always felt off. One day he and his son came to a worship night hoping to be touched by God. I started praying with the father. I prayed that he would have the wisdom not abandon how he was relating to God, but to layer on top new connections in the Spirit. I continued to pray that he could continue to hear God through

Scripture as well as learn to hear from God through the Holy Spirit.

He stopped me mid-prayer and said I had just "read his mail". That was exactly his struggle. He was so happy for this new idea that he could move deeper into the things of God without having to jettison all he had learned before. Moving the idea of approaching God from an 'either/or' paradox his son was presenting to a 'both/and' mentality brought this pastor the freedom to continue his pursuit of the Holy Spirit without being forced to leave behind the truth God had already deposited in him through the Bible.

The pastor's reaction to that prayer was one of the first hints to me that the 'either/or' mindset is failing us as we approach God. I never advocate that a charismatic should throw off their experiences with God and simply study the Word. Nor do I tell a Bible evangelical to put down their Bibles to prayer and worship until God "touches them." Layering one onto the other helps us become true worshipers in spirit and in truth.

Both/And Thinking Brings Freedom

This both/and shift allows freedom of expression during worship, freedom to pursue prophetic utterances, freedom to pursue healing, miracles and all the gifts of God, without abandoning study of the core tenets of the Biblical faith.

Truth and spirit is not an either/or proposition. God said "and" so we need to live in the "and." Many churches and denominations of Christ have an emphasis on spirit or truth: a style of worship, expressions of passion for the Lord, and facets of service for God's people or the community they reach out to.

Each church has its own culture that can be celebrated. For each corporate gathering, the modes of expression, the methods of worship, the timing, tempos and techniques of a corporate service are cultural expressions of the fellowship that is gathering to the Father. It is the merging of spiritual pursuits and seeking truth through the Scriptures that bring about what the Father is seeking: worshipers in spirit and in truth. Let us all become bridges, helping join together the diverse fellowships and expressions found in the Family of God. Let us love and appreciate the keen pursuers of the Bible, those who worship the Father in truth. Let us also love and appreciate those who worship the Father in spirit, with their pursuit of the Holy Spirit's presence and power in their midst. Let's embrace the 'both/and' thinking of a 'two-winged' church, that we may soar in God's Kingdom as we pursue worshiping the Father, together, adding to one another!

Faith in Action

- Visit worship expressions that are different than your regular church and ask the Lord to reveal Himself there.
- Ask the Lord to guide you by His spirit of wisdom and truth, just as much as you search the Scriptures for guidance.
- What does it mean to you to be lead by the law written on your heart?
- What does it mean for you to be a worshiper in spirit?
- What does it mean for you to be a worshiper in truth?

Further Reading

- *Prophetic Community: God's Call for All to Minister in His Gifts*, Dr. Kim Maas 2019
- *Holy Fire: A Balanced, Biblical Look at the Holy Spirit's Work in Our Lives*, RT Kendall 2014
- *The Beginner's Guide to Spiritual Gifts*, Sam Storms 2013

2

LOVE AND POWER

As I described in the introduction, my journey started in Bible-loving evangelical churches for which I still have great love and affection. I am grateful that their earnest appreciation and avid pursuit of the Bible and God became deeply ingrained in me. However, most of the teaching regarding the Holy Spirit I received in these churches was correct but incomplete.

We have already established our twin pursuits of becoming worshippers in both spirit and in truth (John 4:24). Now we will discuss the spiritual and supernatural more fully. The Bible reveals the Holy Spirit, a full and equal Person in the Godhead, as He pertains to the daily life of a follower of Christ. We will begin with a brief overview of the foundational ideas about the work and ministry of the Holy Spirit, particularly, the resurrection of Christ, our new spiritual birth at the time of salvation, and the sealing by the Holy Spirit. If any of these ideas are new to you I suggest some further reading.[2] The Holy Spirit's power should not be the sole pursuit of our

---

2 Holy Spirit, Billy Graham 2011

interaction with the Holy Spirit. But if this pursuit has never been encouraged in your life, then there is a lot of catching up to do.

Of course the Holy Spirit convicts us of sin, regenerates believers, gives wisdom and comfort, and dwells within us. We can guard our relationship *and* engage in a Scriptural pursuit of the powerful gifts that the Bible presents as our portion as followers of Christ. Many fellowships have lost the pursuit of power, miracles and the supernatural aspects of the Holy Spirit. These pursuits should not seem foreign to any of us, as they were definitely not foreign to the early churches established by the disciples.

Foundational Works of the Holy Spirit

We must re-train our minds according to the Bible as we expand our understanding of all that Christ affords us through the Holy Spirit. From Scripture we will lay the foundational basis of the power of the Holy Spirit in our lives and study how God moved in power in the Old Testament and in the life and work of Christ. In the next chapter, we will consider the power of God that is promised and intended for all New Testament believers in all churches.

Many of us take our spiritual inheritance for granted and do not fully access all that Christ paid for at the cross. The powerful and supernatural events of the Bible relay truths about the Holy Spirit's moving in power among the children of God. In Acts 1:8, Jesus says that power and the Holy Spirit will be given to His disciples, so we will look at the initial encounters Christian believers have with power and the Holy Spirit: our belief in the resurrection of Jesus, and the miracle of new life.

Resurrected Christ

By faith we believe in the miracle of the resurrection of Christ. By faith we are saved when we believe Jesus was raised from the dead and we make Him Lord of our lives. No one alive today personally saw or heard Jesus' death and resurrection, yet we still believe in the resurrection miracle, which is a work of the Holy Spirit (Romans 8:11 & 1 Peter 3:18). Our faith is based in the resurrection of Jesus Christ, a victory over death and the grave and the greatest act of miraculous power God has ever worked in the world. All believers share this belief in the power of God.

Ephesians 2:8 reminds us *how* faith saves us: "For by grace you have been saved through faith." Romans 10:9 focuses on *what* we have faith in: "if you confess with your mouth that Jesus is Lord and believe in your heart that God raised him from the dead, you will be saved." This faith leads to the miraculous new life we receive when we believe in Jesus.

New Creation

Salvation is a key spiritual, or supernatural, event in our lives. An incalculable transformation occurs in our heart at the moment of salvation. Our Lord describes this as our new 'spiritual birth,' and Paul wrote extensively about us as a 'new creation' in Christ.

> *"Jesus answered him, "Truly, truly, I say to you, unless one is born again he cannot see the kingdom of God." Nicodemus said to him, "How can a man be born when he is old? Can he enter a second time into his mother's*

> *womb and be born?" Jesus answered, "Truly, truly, I say to you, unless one is born of water and the Spirit, he cannot enter the kingdom of God. That which is born of the flesh is flesh, and that which is born of the Spirit is spirit." John 3:3-6*

The supernatural creation of a reborn spirit happens when we, repenting of our sins, follow Jesus Christ as Lord of our lives. We were dead in spirit, now we are alive. We were only born of flesh, but now we are born in the spirit as well.

Paul describes the same idea as each of us becoming a "new creation" in I Corinthians 5:17: "Therefore, if anyone is in Christ, the new creation has come: The old has gone, the new is here!" It is an error to explain these events as a progression of natural earthly actions. This is a supernatural spiritual creation formed in you. Was salvation just a step up in being a better version of yourself? No, God placed a new creation, a new living spirit, in you. This is an entirely new life found in Christ which is powered by the Holy Spirit. It is a whole new way of living: a brand new life.

You are a spiritual creation made alive again, filled by the Holy Spirit of God, full of life and power. Each of us has our own story of rebirth, our testimony of God's good work in us. Your day of salvation was supernatural, a miracle. Dismissing salvation as a series of 'natural events' diminishes God's miraculous work in regenerating each heart. Your heart that once was dead is now alive in Christ through salvation.

Indwelling Holy Spirit

Jesus promised us the Holy Spirit, and Paul reassured the early churches of this truth. Jesus said in John 14:16-17, "And I will ask the Father, and he will give you another advocate to help you and be with you forever — the Spirit of truth." A few verses later in John 14:26 Jesus promises the Holy Spirit again: "But the Helper, the Holy Spirit, whom the Father will send in my name, he will teach you all things and bring to your remembrance all that I have said to you." The Holy Spirit—helper, advocate, teacher—will be with each of us forever. What a mighty gift!

In letters to the early churches, Paul expounds on the work of the Holy Spirit in us. The Holy Spirit is a seal, a guarantee of God's salvation in us. Ephesians 1:13 reads, "when you heard the word of truth, the gospel of your salvation, and believed in him, were sealed with the promised Holy Spirit." Again 1 Corinthians 1:22 says "and [God] has also put his seal on us and given us his Spirit in our hearts as a guarantee." When we believed in Christ, our hearts were supernaturally locked, guarded, and sealed by the Holy Spirit.

Paul twice reminds the Corinthian church that they have the Holy Spirit and are walking temples of God. 1 Corinthians 3:16 reads, "Do you not know that you are God's temple and that God's Spirit dwells in you?" and 1 Corinthians 6:19 repeats, "Do you not know that your body is a temple of the Holy Spirit within you, whom you have from God?" Paul teaches that the Holy Spirit is in each one of us. This means that each of our bodies is a temple; the Holy Spirit has taken residence in our very bodies! The Holy Spirit of the Almighty God resides in us just as Jesus promised He would. This is the spiritual basis for God's initial interactions with us through faith. The Holy Spirit seeks to be more than an idle observer in our lives. He was given to guide us, to help us, to comfort us. He was given so that we could continue the work of God through us as we will discover as we continue in our journey.

The Love of God

Early in my church planting days, after I had been through years of learning to embrace the power and working of the Holy Spirit, I was still adding to my understanding of what this all truly meant. In pursuing the work of the Holy Spirit I had seen a lot of fanaticism and excess. I was at one of our small prayer gatherings and I commented to a few people that I did not want to be one of 'those Christians' who simply pursued the power of God, but wanted to be known for the love of God. Two people immediately noted that this was a false 'either/or' idea. They refused to accept a separation of the love of God from the power of God. For when God moves in power, it is always rooted and motivated by His love.

God is love, and God loves us. God loves the world. He is love. It is a bedrock tenet of our faith and the very central attribute of God's nature. There are over forty instances of the 'steadfast love' of God, and over eighty instances of the 'steadfast love' of the Lord in Scripture where God speaks of Himself and people praise God as loving, or people direct declarative blessings and prayers to God.

Such declarations and prayers are spread throughout the whole Old Testament, including the poetic Psalms, historical books like 1 & 2 Samuel, and the books of the prophets:

- "**The Lord loves you** and is keeping the oath that he swore to your fathers..." Deuteronomy 7:8
- "Know therefore that the Lord your God is God, the faithful God who keeps covenant and **steadfast love** with those who love him and keep his commandments, to a thousand generations." Deuteronomy 7:9
- "The Lord, the Lord, a God merciful and gracious, slow to anger, and **abounding in steadfast** love and faithfulness." Exodus 34:6
- "But you, Lord, are a compassionate and gracious God, slow to anger, **abounding in love** and faithfulness." Psalms 86:15
- "O Lord, the great and awesome God, who keeps covenant and **steadfast love with those who love him.**" Daniel 4:9
- "The Lord your God is in your midst, a mighty one who will save; **he will rejoice over you with gladness; he will quiet you by his love.**" Zephaniah 3:17

God is a God of love, and is described as such in the Old Testament repeatedly. God presents Himself as a God full of mercy, abounding in steadfast love! The six verses above are but a small sample.

The Gospels and the Epistles contain even more reminders of God's love for us:

- "For **God so loved** the world, that he gave his only Son, that whoever believes in him should not perish but have eternal life." John 3:16
- "Anyone who does not love does not know God, **because God is love**. This is how God showed his love among us: He sent his one and only Son into the world that we might

live through him. This is love: not that we loved God, but that **he loved us and sent his Son** as an atoning sacrifice for our sins." 1 John 4:8-10

- "So we have come to know and to believe **the love that God has for us. God is love**, and whoever abides in love abides in God, and God abides in him." 1 John 4:16
- "See what kind **of love the Father** has given to us, that we should be called children of God." 1 John 3:1
- "But **God shows his love for us** in that while we were still sinners, Christ died for us." Romans 5:8
- "...[nothing] will be able to separate us from the **love of God in Christ Jesus** our Lord." Romans 8:39
- "But God, being rich in mercy, because of **the great love** with which he loved us..." Ephesians 2:4
- "May the Lord direct your hearts to the **love of God** and to the steadfastness of Christ." 2 Thessalonians 3:5

Time and again, the apostles and gospel writers remind us of the love of God. Love is sacrifice, and Jesus died for us. Love is adoption, and God now calls us His children. Love is merciful and kind, and God forgave us. Love provides continual presence and belonging, and God now abides with us forever.

But intellectually knowing God's love is not enough; it is meant to be experienced. Jesus did not just teach on God's love—he demonstrated it. God's love demands action, firstly on His part, and secondly on ours as His primary conduit of love to the world.

Jesus regularly taught His disciples that loving God and loving others were the keys to the Kingdom of God. "You are not far from the Kingdom," He said to a religious leader who responded that loving God was important (Mark 12:29-34). In fact, Jesus sent out His disciples with more than just a message of love. Jesus commanded them: "As you go, proclaim this message: 'The kingdom of heaven has come near.' Heal the sick, raise the dead, cleanse those who have leprosy, drive out demons. Freely you have received; freely give'" Matthew 10:7-8. These were not only loving actions but *powerful* actions.

The Power of God

The power of healings and miracles was used to validate the message of Christ, but it also came from the Father's heart of love. Many churches teach that the power released in Jesus' life was to validate His message or the power in the Apostles' lives was to validate the Bible. Those groups use John 20:30-31, " Now Jesus did many other signs in the presence of the disciples, which are not written in this book; but these are written so that you may believe that Jesus is the Christ, the Son of God, and that by believing you may have life in his name." True, the signs were done that we might believe, but this could not have been His sole motivation because Jesus performed healings due to His compassion as well, as Matthew 14:14 states, "When he went ashore he saw a great crowd, and he had compassion on them and healed their sick."

Christ's love led Him to heal. He did not try to link spiritual truth to the healings. In John 9, Jesus explicitly refuses to make a theology point concerning sin and blindness. Instead His desire was to heal the man so the might of the Father could be displayed (John 9:3). Jesus did not work miracles to back up his teachings. Rather, his miracles support His mission of love, a mission of love that ultimately ended with His sacrifice at the cross.

Paul said he did not preach the gospel with intellectual arguments about God, but with displays of power (1 Corinthians 2:4). Love without demonstration is theory at best, hypocritical or deceitful at worst. True love gives, effects change, and redeems the objects of its love. If love has a desire to give, but is powerless to follow through, what use is that love? Love turned to action is fully formed. God's love is not impotent. It is powerful and mighty.

The link between God's power and His love is strong in Scripture. Zephaniah 3:17 links God's might to His love for people: "The Lord your God is in your midst, a mighty one who will save; he will rejoice over you with gladness; he will quiet you by his love..." In Deuteronomy 4:37, Moses links the power to save the people of Israel from Egypt with His love: "And because he loved your fathers and chose their offspring after them and brought you out of Egypt with his own presence, by his great power." This is great news that we have a God of both love and power to bring His love to tangible action.

God uses His power to rescue and free the people He loves. It is His nature to love, the force of that nature moves in power and miracles. God's love is very effectual. His love wanted to give us new life, and so He did through the loving sacrifice of His Son. Then, through His resurrection, we now have hope in resurrection life, not just in the future but now.

For the rest of this chapter, we will pursue a fuller understanding of how God's love and power come together.

Pursuing Power

In the previous chapter, we focused on the need to pursue God both in truth and in spirit. The interesting thing is that both sides of the spirit and truth dialog can actually miss the need to pursue the power of God.

We come across verses like Matthew 8:32, "and you will know the truth, and the truth will set you free," and think truth is all that is needed to free people from their issues. Likewise, we come across 2 Corinthians 3:17, "where the Spirit of the Lord is, there is freedom,'' and state that if people just had a spiritual encounter with the Holy Spirit, they would be free of all their issues. This type of either/or thinking limits us.

Freedom can come through spirit or truth, or both. But really, spirit and truth are not that far from each other, as we already noted that one name for the Holy Spirit is the Spirit of Truth (John 14:17 & 16:13).

Neither spirit-led groups nor truth-led groups should take the power of God for granted. We shall see in Scripture, that both groups can completely miss the need for the power of God if they are not careful.

While Jesus was in Jerusalem, the last week before his crucifixion and resurrection, some religious leaders tried to trap Him with questions: "That same day the Sadducees, who say there is no resurrection, came to him with a question ... But Jesus answered them, 'You are wrong, because you know neither the Scriptures nor the power of God'" (Matthew 22:22,29). The question is not as interesting as the answer He gave them. Jesus made a distinction between knowing God's Word and knowing God's power. The knowledge of Scripture does not link directly to knowledge of God's power. You can understand one and mistake the other. Or like the Sadducees, you can miss both.

There is also a distinction between the Holy Spirit and power. In Acts 10:38 we see that distinction: "God anointed Jesus of Nazareth with the Holy Spirit and power, and how he went around doing good and healing." I want to pull out the *'and'* between Holy Spirit and power. Being anointed with the Holy Spirit *'and'* being anointed with power are distinctly different things. Paul makes a similar distinction in 1 Thessalonians 1:5, "our gospel came to you not only in word, but also in power and in the Holy Spirit and with full conviction." We must move beyond just the presence of the Holy Spirit in our lives, and make sure that the power of God is also present in our churches and fellowships.

I have known 'spirit-filled' churches that taught on the gifts and power of the Holy Spirit but never actually expected the power of God to be released in their midst. I have also known Bible-focused churches that taught on the gifts of the Spirit, but lacked an expectation of God honoring and fulfilling His word with action and power. I have also seen churches that do not teach on the gifts at all and yet some of them operated powerfully, almost by accident. Thankfully, more and more churches, fellowships, and pastors are reawakening to the truth of seeking the presence, love, and power of God in our lives and in our meetings.

Power of Christ

Let us move to the life, ministry and messages of our Lord found in the Gospels and see love and power at work together.

> *"You know the message God sent to the people of Israel, announcing the good news of peace through Jesus Christ, who is Lord of all. You know what has happened throughout the province of Judea, beginning in Galilee after the baptism that John preached— how God anointed Jesus of Nazareth with the Holy Spirit and power, and how he went around doing good and healing all who were under the power of the devil, because God was with him.*
>
> *"We are witnesses of everything he did in the country of the Jews and in Jerusalem. They killed him by hanging him on a cross, but God raised him from the dead on the third day and caused him to be seen."* Acts 10:36-40

This was Peter's summary of Christ's ministry on earth. When Peter testified to Gentiles for the first time, he highlighted the preaching of good news, the anointing of the Holy Spirit and the anointing of power, Jesus' healing, as well as His death and resurrection. Power and the Holy Spirit was so central in Peter's understanding of Christ's ministry that he includes it in his short two-paragraph summary of Christ's earthly ministry.

Let us review the ministry and message of Christ and receive a similar understanding that Peter had. We will look at the initial arrival of the Holy Spirit upon Jesus, followed by an extended fast of Jesus. Then we will take a take a longer look at the wisdom, teaching and miracles of Jesus.

Jesus' first recorded interaction with the Holy Spirit is at His baptism. During His baptism by John the Baptist, the Holy Spirit descended upon Jesus and remained. All four gospels record this event. John 1:32 says, "John bore witness: "I saw the Spirit descend from heaven like a dove, and it remained on him." Immediately after His baptism, Jesus is led by the Spirit into the desert for 40 days of fasting and temptation. Then in the Gospel of Luke, after Jesus returns from fasting and temptation, the writer notes another outcome of this period. "And Jesus returned in the power of the Spirit to Galilee, and a report about him went out through all the surrounding country." Luke 4:14

He entered the desert with the *presence* of the Holy Spirit, but He left the desert in the *power* of the Spirit. Immediately upon returning in power, Jesus began to teach in the synagogues: first in Nazareth, then in Capernaum. Luke 4:36 captures the people's wonder as they acknowledge His power and authority. "And they were all amazed and said to one another, "What is this word? For with authority and power he commands the unclean spirits, and they come out!" A few verses later Jesus heals all who came to him. "Now when the sun was setting, all those who had any who were sick with various diseases brought them to him, and he laid his hands on every one of them and healed them." Luke 4:40.

Power was a hallmark of Jesus' ministry. Though it was not specifically mentioned in that Luke 4:40 verse, in later chapters His healing ministry is directly linked to His power:

- Luke 5:17 '... and the power of the Lord was with him to heal.'
- Luke 6:19, "And all the crowd sought to touch him, for power came out from him and healed them all,"
- Luke 8:46, "Jesus said, "Someone touched me, for I perceive that power has gone out from me."

The Holy Spirit can move in notable miracles but also in more subtle ways like inspiring wise teachings and other things we do not always ascribe as miraculous. We see Jesus displaying many of the attributes of the Holy Spirit at work. Both the Gospels of Matthew and Mark note that the people of the regions ascribed power to Jesus as well as wisdom. Mark 6:2 says, "he began to teach in the synagogue, and many who heard him were astonished, saying, "Where did this man get these things? What is the wisdom given to him? How are such mighty works done by his hands?" Both the wise teachings and miracles surprised the people. The Holy Spirit at work tends to get people's attention!

By the Spirit of God, Jesus demonstrated both His wisdom and His power for miracles which are listed as spiritual gifts in 1 Corinthians 12. Christ showed us the 'both/and' of truth and spirit worship as he walked in wisdom and power.

Love of Christ

Jesus moved in the power of the Holy Spirit but also we find that all the miracles and gifts of the Spirit were done in love. We know that Jesus sought to administer the love of God. For God is love (1 John 4:8), and the Father is shown through Jesus (John 14:9). So we know that everything He did was motivated by love. In the Gospel of Matthew, directly preceding the multiplication of food for thousands (Matt 14:15-21), we see that Jesus healed many sick. Matthew 14:14 states, "When he went ashore he saw a great crowd, and he had compassion on them and healed their sick." Out of compassion and His love of the people, He healed their sick and fed them. He miraculously multiplied fish because he loved the people. When Jesus saw they were hungry, He displayed the power of God in love by multiplying food.

Furthermore, Father God, who loved the world, sent Jesus to the world to destroy the works of the devil, for this is "the reason the Son of God appeared" (1 John 3:9). John 10:10 says, "The thief comes only to steal and kill and destroy. I [Jesus] came that they may have life and have it abundantly." Jesus had to walk in love and power to fulfill His purpose and demonstrate what the Father was really like.

People did not come to Jesus because He passed out hugs and affirmations. People came to Him because they could be healed, obtain food, or see other powerful miracles, signs, and wonders. We know Jesus created water out of wine, walked on water, raised Lazarus from the dead, calmed a raging storm and exercised authority over demons, all by the power of the Holy Spirit in Him. God's love worked with power to fulfill His mission.

Jesus walked with the Holy Spirit. We see the Holy Spirit moving in His life in power, wise teachings, and other spiritual gifts. But all that Jesus did in power under-girded His love and compassion. He was on a mission of love that required powerful demonstrations of love including physical healings, spiritual freedom from evil spirits, and even the multiplication of food.

Power & Love Comes Home

For years I had been ministering in the love of God by leading small groups and discipling people. This ministry took a lot of time, care, patience, and enduring hope. Most of the time my plans for the ministry could be carried out whether God really showed up or not. There were the breakthroughs in thinking, teaching of doctrine, slow progressive life transformations, and answered prayer requests. But it is very different from a healing ministry or deliverance time; in those, you definitely know when God shows up and when He does not.

I was led by God into this shepherding role in subtle ways. I would pray and write notes about how to lead the small group Bible discussion or I would study the Bible to gain general wisdom I could apply as needed to people's situations. Yet no one would necessarily notice if God did not show up.

Then I was led to go on a mission's trip to Honduras for several weeks with a teaching and healing ministry. I listened as intercessors heard from God and prayed accurately for specific weaknesses, like the covering over our buses; the very next day a gang shootout happened next to one of our buses, but none of the bullets caused harm to our team. I saw and took part as God healed and delivered many in Jesus' name; I wanted to bring this home with me. I heard God call me into new ministry very clearly and had it confirmed through the prayers and prophetic words of other believers over me. I wanted to listen to God better and go home with a renewed relationship. More than ever, I wanted and needed Him to be a part of everything I did.

My expectations of God changed drastically when I saw His love driving His power on that trip. My transformation was immediate and deep. I started to hear God more clearly and more often. He seemed to be leading me and a few others to start a church, giving us step-by-step instructions. We saw the God of power show up in our meetings, in small ways at first, with a few healings and freedom from oppressing spirits.

My heart and desires were changed and the pursuit was on for the power of God. I was longing to see people freed from spiritual oppression and healed from their illnesses. I wanted to partake in all the Lord promised by the Holy Spirit. Will you join me in this pursuit?

Faith in Action

- When sharing God's love through prayer and speech, also seek God in power.
- When between difficult options in a situation, ask the love of God to show up, and for Him to show His power.
- Notice when your first thought is of doing something in love, and shift to a mindset of working in God's power as well.

Further Reading

- *Compelled by Love,* Heidi Baker 2008
- *That None Should Perish - Prayer Evangelism*, Ed Silvoso 1995
- *The Essential Guide to the Power of the Holy Spirit*, Randy Clark 2015

3

POWER IN THE CHURCH

My wife and I were called to a familiar region to start a ministry. At the start of this season, we were organizing and hosting a small worship and ministry night, followed by an outreach the next day. I had invited an out-of-town friend to minister and anchor the evening service. God had been regularly using him to administer the love of God, specifically through healing. He was a rich carrier of God's love and power to everyone he met. At the close of the meeting, the ministry team remained to pray and minister to those wanting prayer.

My friend prayed for one young lady. She started to cry, touched by the love of God. She cried and cried loudly for some time sitting along one wall. The next day she came on the outreach to a small local college. She confessed that she was usually very shy and did not like talking with strangers, especially about God. The touch she received the night before was full of God's love, but it also brought with it a boldness to proclaim God's truth to people on the street. The fruit of that loving touch by God was a powerful boldness to witness for Him.

Her change was like Peter and John who were radically changed by the time they spent with Jesus. After His departure they have an encounter with the Holy Spirit during a prayer meeting. They left that encounter full of boldness.

> *"Now when they saw the boldness of Peter and John, and perceived that they were uneducated, common men, they were astonished. And they recognized that they had been with Jesus. But seeing the man who was healed standing beside them, they had nothing to say in opposition." Acts* 4:13-14

This is one of my favorite verses for a few reasons. First, Jesus' healing power had been recently exhibited in the new church. True, Peter and John had definitely healed people in Jesus' name before this point. But when Jesus had ascended into heaven and He was no longer on earth, His power to heal was still among them. Secondly, it is said that John and Peter were seen as common and uneducated. They were not articulate, well spoken, refined in manner, or otherwise notable people except that they had been with Jesus. Being with Jesus had changed them. These fishermen still talked like fishermen and still had the manners and vocabulary of fishermen. Being with Jesus did not make them more refined like the current religious leaders. They were still "uneducated and common" but they carried the power of Jesus to heal. God's power was active in Jesus. He in turn released His disciples in love and power, and gave them the Holy Spirit.

Jesus Himself promised that we too would walk in the same Spirit that He did. He promised us the Holy Spirit in John 14:15-17 and John 16:13. He expected His disciples to walk in similar power. He expected His disciples to train up more disciples just like them. And promised that all of us should expect the Holy Spirit in our lives. Already we have seen that through Jesus, we are sealed with the Holy Spirit and that we are a temple for the Holy Spirit. But Jesus promised more than just the presence of the Spirit of God in us. And the apostles taught the early churches to expect more than just presence. There was to be power as well.

Encountering Power

In 2014 I went on a mission trip to Honduras. I was excited by everything I was seeing. While I was there God opened up my eyes to His love and His power. Earlier back home, I had been to prayer services and healing meetings where we would pray for back pain and headaches but nobody felt better. But in the meetings in Honduras I truly saw healing miracles and transformed hearts. I saw the true intersection of God's love and power.

The main minister on my trip to Honduras had been teaching from various Scripture passages of God's desire to heal. Faith that God might heal and that He wanted to heal people because of His love began to increase. They were learning that Christ had paid the price for that healing at the cross because of His love and Jesus has the power today to heal us. As the minister concluded teaching, he asked the Holy Spirit to come and work among the people.

This particular evening there were over a thousand people present. I was off to the side watching, as I did not have any ministry duties that evening. I watched an old woman stand with the assistance of the metal walker she had brought. She had the walker in both hands, slowly making her way up front for prayer. After a few steps she pushed the walker slightly out in front, and took one unassisted step, and then grabbed the walker for support. She did this again, pushing it slightly out in front of her and taking one or two steps before grabbing it again for safety.

Her daughter was watching the same thing I was. Each time the old woman pushed the walker in front of her, the daughter's mouth would drop a little. Again the old woman pushed the walker out in front a little further this time, taking three steps before taking a hold of it. Then she pushed it again further still—but this time, she never grabbed the walker again. She shuffled right past it and continued up to the stage without the aid of the walker. By this time the daughter was so shocked and thankful, she was sobbing uncontrollably. The daughter was the one who could not stand after seeing the miracle that had just taken place in her mother. No one could deny that God had just moved in power and that God did this because of His love. The power and love of God were tangibly displayed in this one miraculous healing.

I was changed by this event. I desperately wanted to see the love of God and the power of God move to touch people. The next morning during prayer, I asked the Lord to see everything I saw on this trip to happen in my hometown of San Jose, California. I felt like God met me immediately in that prayer and by the time I got home I was already planning to start a new ministry grounded in the love and power of God.

The apostle Peter, when reflecting on the ministry of Jesus, encouraged the churches regarding the power of God in Jesus. 2 Peter 1:3 states, "His divine power has given us everything we need for a godly life." The apostle Paul spoke much about the power of Jesus, and we will review those verses more when we look at the power of the Holy Spirit in every believer.

Power of the Holy Spirit

Earlier we reviewed and saw that we when received salvation through Jesus Christ, we also received the Spirit (John 14:16-17), were sealed by the Spirit (Ephesians 1:13, 1 Corinthians 1:22) and even became a temple of God with the Spirit inside us (1 Corinthians 3:16). The Holy Spirit's presence in our hearts was not the only intended outcome of our salvation. We have righteousness, comfort, and peace by the same Spirit in us as well.

But Jesus promised more, and the early church teachers expected more as a result of the indwelling Spirit; they expected power. As we review Christ's promise and the apostles' early encouragements, we will recapture the promise of power through the Holy Spirit. This sets the stage for us to actively pursue the spiritual gifts that were to be administered in all churches and disciples of Jesus Christ.

Power in the Apostles

In Acts we can see the religious leaders at that time had an incomplete understanding regarding power because they were amazed that Peter was able to walk in such power. In Acts 3, there is the amazing story of Peter healing a lame man in the name of Jesus Christ. Preaching to the temple crowds the salvation through Christ, Peter said, "Men of Israel, why do you wonder at this, or why do you stare at us, as though by our own power or piety we have made him walk?" Act 3:12. Peter knew it was the power of God, not his own power. But in Acts 4:7 the leaders ask by what "power" Peter did that miracle, which shows that the religious leaders of the time could not fathom how the power of God could be working through a person.

This story of Peter is after the giving of the Holy Spirit at Pentecost and Peter was now exhibiting the power of God, just as Jesus did. Jesus promised all of His disciples that they would receive the Holy Spirit and power, as Acts 1:8 says, "But you will receive power when the Holy Spirit has come upon you, and you will be my witnesses in Jerusalem and in all Judea and Samaria, and to the end of the earth." This includes all of us who believe in Him today. The old religious leaders might have missed God's power, but we should not.

In John 14:12, Jesus says, "Truly, truly, I say to you, whoever believes in me will also do the works that I do; and greater works than these will he do, because I am going to the Father." The word "works" here in the original text means "business," "occupation," or "employment," not a single act, effort or work, but the ongoing employment or profession of a person. In our modern vocabulary, it could be said that He was constantly preoccupied with the Father's work.

Jesus was saying that just as His regular business was teaching, healing, casting out unclean spirits, and drawing people to the Father, so should that be our regular activity or preoccupation. Simply put, Jesus' life model was to only do what the Father was doing (Matthew 5:19). Peter was about the activities Jesus instilled in him. Peter was healing the sick and preaching salvation in Jesus. Peter was not the only one displaying the power of God, nor was the power limited to only the twelve Apostles of Jesus.

Power in the Disciples

The mandate to continue the works of Jesus comes to all His disciples, not just the twelve Apostles, and we see some early examples of this in Acts. In Acts 6:2-6, the apostles needed to appoint some of the disciples to special service roles which came with a commissioning of prayer and laying on of hands.

> *"And the twelve summoned the full number of the disciples and said, "It is not right that we should give up preaching the word of God to serve tables. Therefore, brothers, pick out from among you seven men of good repute, full of the Spirit and of wisdom, whom we will appoint to this duty. But we will devote ourselves to prayer and to the ministry of the word." And what they said pleased the whole gathering, and they chose Stephen, a man full of faith and of the Holy Spirit, and Philip, and Prochorus, and Nicanor, and Timon, and Parmenas, and Nicolaus, a proselyte of Antioch. These they set before the apostles, and they prayed and laid their hands on them." Acts 6:2-6*

Stephen and Philip are noted as two of the men full of the Spirit and of wisdom in Acts 6:5. The Apostles laid hands on them and prayed for them. Immediately after, Act 6:8 reads, "And Stephen, full of grace and power, was doing great wonders and signs among the people." Philip also moved in power in Acts 8 when he traveled to Samaria. As he worked in power, signs and miracles followed him, so that "They all paid attention to him, from the least to the greatest, saying, "This man is the power of God that is called Great" (Acts 8:10), and "Even

Simon [the sorcerer] himself believed, and after being baptized he continued with Philip. And seeing signs and great miracles performed, he was amazed" (Acts 8:13).

Ananias is another disciple who is used by God to administer healing to Paul in Damascus in Acts 9. He is not listed as an Apostle, nor did he write any books of the Bible. He was simply a man going about the works of God. We see that it was not just the super twelve Disciples having the power of God but many other disciples. What was encouraged and open to those disciples, should be encouraged and open to us.

Power in all Believers

Beyond these historical stories in Acts of disciples having or using the power of God, we can gain great encouragement for our own lives, families, and churches by looking at how the earlier churches were formed and taught one another.

We have already looked at the verses where Jesus promises the Helper, the Holy Spirit. At the end of Luke and the beginning of Acts, Jesus explicitly links the Holy Spirit's coming with an endowment of power. Luke 24:49 says, "And behold, I am sending the promise of my Father upon you. But stay in the city until you are clothed with power from on high." Act 1:8 states, "But you will receive power when the Holy Spirit has come upon you, and you will be my witnesses in Jerusalem and in all Judea and Samaria, and to the end of the earth." Both these statements were given to a large group of disciples, who would then gather in an upper room for prayer on the day of Pentecost to receive the Holy Spirit.

Purposes of Power

God demonstrates that He lends His power to those in need. Reviewing Scripture will quickly reveal a few purposes for when and why God reveals His power. Knowing God's ways with regards to His displays of power will help guide and encourage us as we set the bounds for walking with the Holy Spirit in power. From providing actual physical strength to Samson in Judges, to providing persevering endurance, to working miracles through with His power, we see the God aiding those who call upon Him. We will look at a few examples now.

Twice in Isaiah 40, we see God granting strength and power: "He gives power to the faint, and to him who has no might he increases strength" (Isaiah 40:29) and "they who wait for the LORD shall renew their strength; they shall mount up with wings like eagles; they shall run and not be weary; they shall walk and not faint" (Isaiah 40:31). We know this is partly poetic speech, but the point is God strengthens those who depend on him.

The prophet Micah says, "But as for me, I am filled with power, with the Spirit of the LORD, and with justice and might, to declare to Jacob his transgression and to Israel his sin" (Micah 3:8), making an explicit connection between being filled with power and the Spirit of God.

What once was a rare occasion before Christ is now an everyday expectation for those in Christ. Taking a deeper look at a few of these examples of power will solidify our understanding of God's ways and provide context in our journey with the Holy Spirit.

Power to Save

It is excellent news that we have the same Spirit of power that raised Christ from the dead living inside each of us who believe. As Romans 8:11 says, "If the Spirit of him who raised Jesus from the dead dwells in you, he who raised Christ Jesus from the dead will also give life to your mortal bodies through his Spirit who dwells in you." Praise the Lord for the life that we are given through His Spirit in us.

Writing to the church in Rome, Paul reminds them that the gospel of Christ has the power of salvation, exclaiming, "For I am not ashamed of the gospel, for it is the power of God for salvation to everyone who believes" (Romans 1:16). Paul says it again to the church in Corinth in two different letters. Here are three different passages regarding God's power to save us:

- For the word of the cross is folly to those who are perishing, but **to us who are being saved it is the power of God** (1 Corinthians 1:18)
- And God raised the Lord and will also **raise us up by his power** (1 Corinthians 6:14)
- For he was crucified in weakness, but lives by the power of God. For we also are weak in him, but in dealing with you we will **live with him by the power of God** (2 Corinthians 13:4)

These verses form a great foundation for us to understand we already walk in God's power. We were saved, raised up, and now live by the power of God. This is the truth in Scripture.

Power for Each Day

God's power in our lives does not end with the work of salvation. We are to know and experience God's power as we live life. Both the apostles Peter and Paul frequently reminded the early churches of this truth. Peter, broadly addressing all believers, acknowledges that we are guarded by God's power (1 Peter 1:5), and states that we serve by the strength God gives us, "whoever speaks, as one who speaks oracles of God; whoever serves, as one who serves by the strength that God supplies—in order that in everything God may be glorified through Jesus Christ" (1 Peter 4:11).

Three times in his letter to the Ephesians, Paul spoke of God's ongoing power in our lives. He encouraged them to be strong with the strength of God (Ephesians 6:10) and prayed "that you may know ...what is the immeasurable greatness of his power toward us who believe, according to the working of his great might." (Ephesians 1:18-19). Paul interceded that God would give them a greater understanding of the great power already working in them. We too need a revelation of God's power in us. We grow more confident to do His will and feel more assured to accomplish His work when we know His power comes alongside us each and every day.

The verse Ephesians 3:20, "Now to him who is able to do far more abundantly than all that we ask or think, according to the power at work within us," reminds us that God "is able" to do many more wonderful things than we could ask or imagine. It is a wonderful reminder to know God can and will do abundant works for us, but the avenue of these works is the power of His Spirit that is within us. The Holy Spirit and His power is in us already!

Many times we want God to fulfill the promise in Ephesians 3:20 by working a miracle from heaven. We want him to move or change our circumstances. Check the verse again. Maybe we need to look inside to the power that is already within us to overcome the obstacles in front of us.

Faith is the key. We do not drum up the power of God by effort or demand it from God because of good works. Just as we receive new life by faith, so too we receive the power of God by faith. Galatians 3:5 challenges us accordingly: "Does he who supplies the Spirit to you and works miracles among you do so by works of the law, or by hearing with faith...?" We did not receive the Spirit by works and we do not receive power for perseverance or miracles by works.

We should all be encouraged that we can be strong in the Lord by his might even today and that His power is at work inside each of us, every day, accomplishing more than we ever asked or thought.

Power to Persevere

Often when we hear the phrase "the power of God" we immediately think of miracles. But the power of God in Scripture is exemplified through the lives of persevering believers much more than through stunning miracles. We will begin by looking at how God gives us power for perseverance and focus later on the spiritual gifts given by the Holy Spirit. Knowing Christ and the power of his resurrection comes with sharing in his sufferings. A partial review of Scripture will help establish this point:

- "that I may know him and the power of his resurrection, and may share his sufferings" (Philippians 3:10)
- "Therefore do not be ashamed of the testimony about our Lord, nor of me his prisoner, but share in suffering for the gospel by the power of God" (2 Timothy 1:8)
- "we have not ceased to pray for you [to be] strengthened with all power, according to his glorious might, for all endurance and patience with joy" (Colossians 1:11)
- "For this I [Paul] toil, struggling with all his energy that he powerfully works within me" (Colossians 1:29)

Do you see how power and suffering are mentioned together in these verses? God gave Paul more strength to endure struggles, and Paul also prays that we too would have the power to endure, suffer, and fulfill every good work through the power of God's Spirit.

To the church of Thessalonica, Paul prays "that our God may make you worthy of his calling and may fulfill every resolve for good and every work of faith by his power" (Thessalonians 1:11). The early churches were not told to rest in a power that only gives new life, but to trust in an ongoing power from God that helps us endures suffering and shares in the troubles for the gospel.

In another portion of scripture, Paul encourages his spiritual son, Timothy, not to fear. 2 Timothy 1:7 states, "for God gave us a spirit not of fear but of power and love and self-control." Paul mentions three things that counteract fear which come from the Holy Spirit in us: love, self control, and power! Paul exhorts Timothy to walk properly in life, through the power, love and self control provided through the Holy Spirit.

The apostle Paul encouraged the early churches to depend on

the Holy Spirit for power. Ephesians 3:16 states "that according to the riches of his glory he may grant you to be strengthened with power through his Spirit in your inner being," and Romans 15:13 reads, "May the God of hope fill you with all joy and peace in believing, so that by the power of the Holy Spirit you may abound in hope." This power from God is not just for our physical bodies, but for our inner being. Our soul, mind and spirit can and should be strengthened by God.

Power for Miracles

The Holy Spirit not only gives us power for living and perseverance, but also power for miracles: "...to another the working of miracles, to another prophecy, to another the ability to distinguish between spirits" (1 Corinthians 12:10), and again in verse 28, "And God has appointed in the church first apostles, second prophets, third teachers, then miracles, then gifts of healing, helping, administrating, and various kinds of tongues." In both verses, the word "miracles" comes from the Greek noun for power. Miracles are, in a strong sense, literally "works of power." In 1 Corinthians 12, Paul reminds one of the early churches to look for the Holy Spirit to give spiritual gifts that include works of power, or miracles. This giving of power promised by Jesus was not to be limited to just the initial 12 Apostles. Our earlier review considered disciples who were not apostles but were working in power and miracles.

Galatians 3:5 talks about the God who "supplies the Spirit to you and works miracles among you." See the distinction between the supplying of the Spirit and the working of miracles. It is very important to note that when God "works miracles among you," this phrasing refers to an ongoing working of miracles in the midst of the church, not just while the apostle preached to them. Paul did not say that God "gave the Spirit" and "worked miracles," but that God supplies and works among them—present, ongoing actions. God was still at work among Galatians at the time that Paul wrote the letter to them.

The entire church was told to expect the Holy Spirit to show up in power in various ways when they met together. Prophecy should be active in their meetings. Healings and miracles should be expected in their fellowships. Wisdom, knowledge, discernment, and speaking and interpreting tongues should all be present in their gatherings. Likewise we should have an expectation in all church fellowships of the Holy Spirit moving in our midst today.

"For I will not venture to speak of anything except what Christ has accomplished through me to bring the Gentiles to obedience—by word and deed, by the power of signs and wonders, by the power of the Spirit of God—so that from Jerusalem and all the way around to Illyricum I have fulfilled the ministry of the gospel of Christ" (Romans 15:18-19). Finally, we should expect miracles when we evangelize. We are to preach the word and demonstrate the word when we take the gospel of Christ to the world. Paul in 1 Corinthians 2:4-5 also states that the gospel they would receive in faith was not built upon words, but the power of God: "my speech and my message were not in plausible words of wisdom, but in demonstration of the Spirit and of power, so that your faith might not rest in the wisdom of men but in the power of God."

Shifting our Thinking

The clear reading of all these Scriptures shows God's power is in us, each and every one of us who are His disciples. God's power resides in us; to think or feel otherwise is to contradict Scripture. God's power in each of us, through the Holy Spirit, helps us to persevere, to present the gospel in word and in powerful deeds, and to serve each other through spiritual gifts.

Do you believe power resides in you? Did the Holy Spirit only deposit power in other people? Do you eagerly desire all gifts and displays of His power to work through you?

For some, it is like those superhero movies when the character starts understanding they have strange new powers. In the movies, there tends to be an initial catalyst for power; which might have been a spider bite, or a green chemical spill, or a bath in glowing blue light. Then they start figuring out they were changed and endowed with power. A new destiny opens up in front of them. Things they did not think were possible now become probable. A new calling dawns upon their minds.

This is actually true for every follower of Christ. We have the resurrection life of Christ in us the moment we are saved and created anew. We have the new mind and righteousness of our Lord. We also have the Spirit of the living God in our hearts, full of wisdom and full of power! The power that raised Christ from the dead is in us through the Holy Spirit, which is better than any superhero's power. But we have to learn about this power, grow in faith and exercise that power of God.

One reason we are aiming high concerning both the presence and power of the Holy Spirit is because if we aim low we will miss out on a portion of what God wants for us. If we miss the power of the Holy Spirit, we are neglecting healing, miracles, and gifts of faith for signs and wonders. Then, if we are not careful, and we lose the teaching and practice of the power of the Holy Spirit, we can start losing connection with the Spirit of truth. If we limit what the Spirit can do in our lives, it can start to limit our theology and thus limit the Spirit and truth in our lives."When the Spirit of truth comes, he will guide you into all the truth" John 16:13a. We need the fullness of the Holy Spirit to guide us into truth.

The notion that God's power in us should move us into a deeper faith that changes our actions and expectations. Both our expectations of God, and our expectations of ourselves as we live for Him. Let us continue to pursue the presence of God and match that pursuit for the power of God in our lives.

Part Two of this book will focus on pursuing the gifts afforded us through the Holy Spirit. We will develop what Christ in us should look like, supernatural theology of an everyday expectation that the Holy Spirit in us should be powerfully active in all parts of our lives. Before embarking on that journey, we will spend the next chapter looking at we how we may initially pursue and stir up the gifts of the Spirit.

Faith in Action

- Ask the Lord to remind you of a memory of the power of God in your life. Use that memory to you start expecting similar situations to arise where God will give you strength and power.
- A miracle is a "work of power." Ask the Lord if there was a recent time you could have asked Him to do a miracle through you.
- Testimonies. Read missionary or revival history books

where God's power was on display. These will build your faith.

- Word and deed. When you want to share the gospel in words, try to also ask the Lord to reveal the gospel through the work of the Holy Spirit as well.

Further Reading

- *God's General - The Revivalists*, Roberts Liardon 2008
- *The Presence & Work of the Holy Spirit*, R. A. Torrey 2004
- *Do What Jesus Did*, Robby Dawkins 2013

4

IMPARTATION

A few years ago I encountered God while I was reading a book on healing and the Holy Spirit. At the time, I was in a church community that was pressing into all the gifts of the Holy Spirit, so I was studying all I could. In a chapter regarding the increase of faith and spiritual gifts, a few pages were dedicated to receiving more gifting by having others pray for you. The book encouraged asking people who were actively using their gifts to pray for you for more of that gifting. God challenged me on a point that I had overlooked completely in my study of the Bible. The book quoted Hebrews 6:1-2 on the instruction about laying on hands.

I was familiar with this passage, for I had taught my small groups that they had to know the six foundational theological statements in Hebrews 6:1-2. How had I missed understanding the importance of and practice of one of them? In asking God about this truth, I felt like He said, "do you know anything of this foundational truth, the laying on of hands?"

I admitted to myself that I did not really know much about this topic. Actually I had no practical experience regarding the laying on of hands. Even though I had read the words of these six doctrines, I had always skipped this one, seeing it as trivial in comparison to the others. I never had the internal curiosity or external challenge to learn and live out the doctrine of "laying on of hands." This was humbling as God confronted me. But there was more humbling coming, because God was not yet done speaking to me.

Next I felt God spoke to my heart, "because of your pride you do not believe you need anything from others. That is why you have resisted having people lay hands on you and pray for you." This was tough for me to swallow. I had dealt with various points of pride in my life for years, and I had thought I was finally doing well on this front. But as He challenged me, I remembered that I would look down on people who would rush around a Christian conference trying to get all the "right people" to pray from them. They would say the reason for their enthusiasm to receive prayer from those people was that "they have something I want." I would think, or straight up tell those people, "well, ask God for what you want; He is the one who can give it to you."

God mightily challenged this perspective. He pointed out that due to my ignorance and pride, I had been missing something He wanted to give me. This brief, but pointed, interaction is one of the core turning points in my life. Of course, not everyone resists laying on of hands because of pride or feeling that they do not need anything from anyone but God Himself. Among other issues, they may resist because of fear, indifference, or lack of context for this practice.

I share this story because deep in me was a true desire to know more of His ways. I wanted to receive a greater portion of His love, His wisdom and gifts so that I could serve Him well.

I wanted to make His Name great in my region. You probably share this desire to know and actively partner with God more. Desiring more of God, more of His Spirit, is never a passion that should be ignored, dissipated, or chastised in ourselves or others. We should all want to be more like Christ, to have His mind, His righteousness, and His love and power to affect the world.

More of the Holy Spirit

In the earliest days of the church we see God pouring out His Spirit on His people. Acts 2 recounts the great outpouring of the Holy Spirit at Pentecost, so that"they were all filled with the Holy Spirit..." (Acts 2:4). The widespread giving of the Holy Spirit to Christ's disciples marks the beginning of the Church, the universal gathering of saints, with Christ as the head. Now, when new believers come into the faith of Christ, they are sealed with the Holy Spirit and become His temple. The Holy Spirit is a promise of God for every believer.[3]

In Acts 4, the religious leaders threatened Peter and John and told them not to preach in Jesus' name anymore. Of course the apostles would not abide by such a command and immediately called a prayer meeting. After their prayers, God moved and shook the building around them, and "they were all **filled with the Holy Spirit** and continued to speak the word of God with boldness" (Acts 4:31).

---

[3] A great many books have been written regarding the full significance of what we receive when the Holy Spirit comes into our lives. This book is not trying to make another entry into those controversial discussions. My focus is to be a voice bridging the "spirit" and "truth" camps into a more unified family under God.

Surely Peter and John had already received the Holy Spirit. Jesus breathed the Spirit on them (John 20:22) and of course they had been filled at Pentecost (Acts 2). Many of the other disciples at this prayer meeting in Acts 4 had probably been in the upper room at Pentecost as well. Did they lose the Holy Spirit? Had they become empty of the Holy Spirit? Had the securing seal of salvation gone missing? Had their access to the Spirit of God vanished? Of course not. The simplest, most straightforward way to understand the Acts 4 filling of the Holy Spirit is that each of the disciples received **more** of God's Spirit, becoming more bold than they were before. In Acts 2, the early church had grown, but by Acts 4, they faced persecution and threats from the same leaders that crucified Jesus. In response to prayer, God gave another filling of the Holy Spirit. God gave more of Himself to them. When it comes to God, there is always more of Him to receive.

Regardless of the position you hold regarding receiving the Holy Spirit or the infilling or baptism of the Holy Spirit, it should be obvious that we should always want more. If the early church in Acts 4 was already filled by the Spirit of God at Pentecost, and could be filled again by the Holy Spirit, we too should seek to be filled more and more by the Spirit of God. People who get hung up on whether or not they have received the first infilling of the Holy Spirit sometimes miss the point of more. Let's simply pursue more of God, always.

In this chapter, we will continually revisit this idea of receiving more of the Holy Spirit. First, we need Him more as we press in for spiritual gifts. Secondly, one of the main modes for an increase in the Spirit is through the laying on of hands, which is otherwise known as impartation.

Laying on of Hands in the Old Testament

Hebrews 6:1-2 claims that "the laying on of hands" is an "elementary doctrine," yet the passage does not expound upon it. This teaching was so taken for granted by the churches receiving this instruction that a single mention was all that was needed to encourage or correct them.

Until God challenged me, I had never heard a sermon on "the laying on of hands" or impartation. However, I had seen laying on of hands a few times during commissioning services when a new pastor was hired to lead the church or when sending out a missions team or a long-term missionary. It really felt like a cultural "we are in this together" moment. No doctrinal or theological significance was ever attached to the gesture. At a couple of conferences I had seen some people really want prayer or laying on of hands from the main speaker; but I wrote those people off as fanatical. It was like going to a concert where everyone wanted a picture with the lead singer. I did not attach much significance to the act.

But for the early Jewish Christians that circulated the book of Hebrews among their churches, they would have been well acquainted with this idea from their history and customs. We can quickly regain their understanding by reviewing a few verses in the Old Testament.

A Sign of Transfer

We see in the book of Leviticus that the laying on of hands was associated with giving sacrifices, specifically sacrifices connected to the removal of sin or guilt. The person offering the sacrifice would lay their hands on the animal before the shedding of its blood as a sign of transferring their sin and iniquity to the animal. This physical touch was not practiced in other types of sacrifices and offerings, like yearly festival offerings, tithes, and gifts to the Lord. We see the phrase "He shall lay his hand on the head of the burnt offering" or a similar rendering in Leviticus 1:4, Leviticus 3:2, Leviticus 4:4,4:15, 4:24, 4:29 and 4:33.

We know now that this practice was a foreshadowing of our sins' transference to the perfect Lamb of God, Jesus, who carried the transgressions and sins for us. The key is that in the Old Testament, the laying on of hands represented a symbolic transfer or impartation of sin from the person who brought the sacrifice to the animal.

A Signal of Commissioning

The other reason for laying hands on a person or group in the Old Testament is for commissioning them. For example, during the ordination of the Levites to set them apart (in other words, making them holy) for the work of God, the congregation of Israel laid hands on the Levites in Numbers 8:10. Similarly, Moses commissioned Joshua in front the people of Israel: "so the LORD said to Moses, 'Take Joshua the son of Nun, a man in whom is the Spirit, and lay your hand on him; make him stand before Eleazar the priest and all of the congregation, and you shall commission him in their sight'" (Numbers 27:18-19).

In the case of the Levites, the laying on of hands by the people was more a communal recognition that they were set apart. For Joshua, Moses laying hands on him was a commission and also a succession of leadership. The people accepted the leadership change and followed Joshua as they had followed Moses.

For Impartation

Deuteronomy 34:9 recounts the same story at the death of Moses, but with an additional detail. "Now Joshua son of Nun was filled with the spirit of wisdom because Moses had laid his hands on him. So the Israelites listened to him and did what the Lord had commanded Moses." This verse links being filled with the spirit of wisdom to the act of Moses laying hands on Joshua. Something more was added; an impartation.

There is another such impartation in the story of the prophets of Elijah and Elisha in 2 Kings 2:15: "Now when the sons of the prophets who were at Jericho saw him opposite them, they said, 'The spirit of Elijah rests on Elisha.'" The spirit that rested on Elijah transferred to Elisha. Though this was not done by the laying on of hands, the principle is the same in that God's Spirit or power can be transferred from one person to another.

Lastly in the book of Numbers, we see God sovereignly impart some of the Spirit that rested on Moses onto the elders of Israel.

> *"So Moses went out and told the people the words of the Lord. And he gathered seventy men of the elders of the people and placed them around the tent. Then the Lord came down in the cloud and spoke to him, and took* ***some of the Spirit that was on him and put it on the seventy elders.*** *And as soon as the Spirit rested on them, they prophesied. But they did not continue doing it." Numbers 11:24-25*

In this story, as in all acts of impartation, God is the chief actor. But God also uses people to transfer authority, power or His Spirit upon another person.

Laying on of Hands in the New Testament

In the New Testament we continue to see examples of laying on of hands and imparting the Spirit of God. The core teaching of laying of hands and impartation is found in the writings to the early church, but let us first stop and review the ministry of Jesus.

In His ministry of healing, Jesus regularly laid hands on men and women. He also welcomed the children and blessed them while laying hands on them. Mark 10:14-16 makes this clear. "'... Let the children come to me; do not hinder them, for to such belongs the kingdom of God. Truly, I say to you, whoever does not receive the kingdom of God like a child shall not enter it.' And he took them in his arms and blessed them, **laying his hands on them**." Jesus wanted to bless them and so laid hands on them

Later we see Jesus transferring power to his twelve disciples, giving them "authority over unclean spirits, to cast them out, and to heal every disease and every affliction" (Matthew 10:1). Mark 6:7 and Luke 9:1 recount the same story of Jesus imparting authority to His disciples. This transfer of authority from Jesus to the twelve apostles was important enough to be retold in three of the four gospels.

Then in Luke 10, Jesus sends out 70 disciples in pairs with specific instructions on how to minister in faith. Upon their return, they were full of joy because the demons obeyed them when they used the name of Jesus. Jesus' response is found in verse 19: "I have **given you authority** to trample on snakes and scorpions and to overcome all the power of the enemy; nothing will harm you." Jesus gave them authority just as he had to the apostles. Jesus' impartation of authority and power extends all the way to us in the present day.

We are not told how Jesus imparted His authority to the 12 disciples or to the 70, but obviously He did. Maybe He prayed for them. Maybe He blessed them. Maybe he laid hands on them. Regardless, those disciples started healing people and casting out demons. In another instance, Jesus did not lay hands on anyone, but simply breathed on them, saying "Receive the Holy Spirit," (John 20:22), and it was done. Impartation can be accomplished more ways than just the laying on of hands. Even though we have not gotten to the early church yet, we have already seen the giving of the Holy Spirit accomplished in a variety of ways. Moses laid hands on Joshua and the Spirit of God increased in Joshua. Elisha traveled with Elijah and was near him when he was taken into heaven, and Elisha was given a double portion of the Spirit that Elijah had. Jesus simply spoke forth His authority or breathed on his disciples who then received more.

Laying on of Hands in Acts

The mention of laying on of hands in Hebrews 6:1-2 was instruction for the early church. The early church did not restart the practice of laying on hands for sacrifices, for Jesus put an end to the need for sacrifices. But the church did continue laying on hands for impartation and commissioning, such as in Acts 6:6, which records an instance of laying on of hands while commissioning the first deacons in the first months of the early church. Immediately after receiving prayer and commissioning from the apostles, Stephen receives grace, power, and the ability to work signs and wonders (Acts 6:8). Then in Acts 8, another commissioned deacon, Philip, goes to

Samaria and works signs, casts out demons, and preaches the gospel. Acts 8:14-17 explicitly links the giving of the Holy Spirit to the laying on of hands.

> *"Now when the apostles at Jerusalem heard that Samaria had received the word of God, they sent to them Peter and John, who came down and prayed for them that they might receive the Holy Spirit, for he had not yet fallen on any of them, but they had only been baptized in the name of the Lord Jesus. Then they laid their hands on them and they received the Holy Spirit."*
> *Acts 8:14-17*

Here in the earliest days of the church we see a direct correlation between the laying on of hands, and the Spirit of God imparted through this act.

Acts 19:6 captures another instance where a group of believers had only been partially baptized. This time only for repentance along the pattern of John the Baptist, but they had not been baptized fully in the name of the Father, the Son and the Holy Spirit. So the apostle Paul comes to this group of disciples and prays for them, and lays hands on them. Then Acts 19:6 records, "And when Paul had laid his hands on them, the Holy Spirit came on them".

Before moving on from the Book of Acts, there is one more story: the healing of Saul (who would become Paul). In Acts 9:17 it says "so Ananias departed and entered the house. And laying his hands on him he said, 'Brother Saul, the Lord Jesus who appeared to you on the road by which you came has sent me so that you may regain your sight and be filled with the Holy Spirit.'" In this single verse we see two common reasons for the laying on of hands in the New Testament. The first is in connection to a prayer for healing. The second is for the filling of the Holy Spirit. We see Paul, still called Saul at this point in the story, on the receiving side of the laying on of hands, both for healing and to receive the Holy Spirit. Later in his ministry, he will be the one used by God to give through the laying on of hands.

Laying on of Hands in the Epistles

Three different times Paul writes to churches or ministering leaders regarding the laying on of hands for impartation. From his time being lead by Christ, and ministering to the people of God, Paul knew God's ways regarding the laying on of hands. To the Roman church, Paul writes, "For I long to see you, that **I may impart to you some spiritual gift** to strengthen you" (Romans 1:11) Paul knew that if he could visit the church in Rome, he could impart gifts of God through his prayers and hands. He understood this mode of God because he had experienced it when he received prayer from Ananias. Also, he had seen it at work in the lives of his spiritual children, like Timothy.

In writing Timothy, Paul sought to encourage him. In both both letters to Timothy, Paul references a commission service where elders laid hands on Timothy and blessed him. Paul writes, "do not neglect the gift you have, which was given you by prophecy when the council of elders laid their hands on you" (1 Timothy 4:14). A spiritual gift was deposited in Timothy when the elders of the church prayed and placed their hands on him as spiritual leaders. Paul reminds Timothy of the same thing again in his next letter: "for this reason I remind you to fan into flame the gift of God, which is in you through the laying on of my hands" (2 Timothy 1:6). This spiritual gift seemed to have been given to Timothy at a later time than when he became a follower of Christ.

God is intentional in His ways. He longs to gather His people into a family, a cohesive, interconnected people of God. Communion is practiced in groups. We are told to bear each other's burdens. It is impossible to baptize oneself; it must be done in fellowship. The spiritual gifts are given for "the common good" of all (1 Corinthians 12:7). Imparting spiritual gifts through the laying on of hands is a key way that God binds us together. At times, what I need from God will only come to me when I am humble to receive through the community of believers what God intends for me to have.

Seeking the Laying on of Hands

Gladly, my story of God chastising me ends with a blessing from Him. I have already mentioned that when God challenged me regarding impartation, it was a turning point in my life. After I humbled myself regarding my need for others to pray for me, God spoke in my heart again, "If you go on one of the upcoming mission trips, I will catch you up with all you have missed so far."

I had just become acquainted with a missions organization that regularly took trips to Brazil, Central America, and other regions and nations. God was asking me to walk with obedience and do what I had always looked down on people for doing: chase after a blessing from another person. Four months later in the summer of 2014, I had the chance to go on a missions trip to Honduras. This trip led by a leader who helped oversee a large revival in the 1990s. The whole trip I stayed in a receiving posture, full of faith and expectation. I was looking for God to touch me and fill me up in ways I had not been filled before.

I had two reasons for being full of faith. First, since I had been studying the laying on of hands I had a much better grasp of its Biblical foundation (everything I just outlined in this chapter). I truly believed from Scripture that God wanted to bless me through the prayers of other men and women. Secondly, I had a specific promise from God that He was going to touch me; He even said He would catch me up for all the times I had missed out earlier. And He really did. God's grace is so amazing!

Over a three day span in the middle of the trip, God touched me repeatedly through the prayers and laying on of hands by multiple men and women of God. One evening a lady prayed and prophesied over me for over a long period. Those words were so encouraging, so comforting, and so endowed with the love of God that I am still being touched and guided by those words years later.

Three different times the head of the ministry or one of the core team leaders prayed over me and I was radically touched. They appeared to see a giant spiritual target on me and just kept praying for me. God's voice seemed louder after they laid hands on me. I saw visions of God bringing revival to my home region. I had the strongest sense I have ever felt that God was truly with me. Sometimes I cried deeply. Other times I trembled so much I could not stand. This touch of God's power and love was very different than anything I had experienced before.

I have since gone on other mission trips and conferences. I have received prayer and let pastors and leaders lay hands on me. But that trip, when God said I would catch up, contained the most impactful couple days I have had receiving deeply from the Lord. Through the hands — the literal hands of women and men — I was filled with a greater portion of God's Spirit than ever before.

The laying on of hands is not merely a symbolic gesture. It is a core elementary doctrine, and we should continue its practice with earnest faith. We should be eager like Paul. He wanted to visit the churches he established so he might impart more spiritual gifts. Likewise, we should want to impart what we have to others. God still uses His people to bless His people. Just as we do communion together, and baptize each other, we also need one another to impart spiritual gifts throughout the Body of Christ. Through the laying on of hands, we stir up the Spirit in us and bless each other with the love and power of God.

Faith in Action

- Check your heart. Have you resisted allowing people to lay hands or impart a blessing on you for any reason?
- Is there an elder, pastor, or small group leader who could stir up your spiritual gifts?
- Is there anyone you are drawn to pray and lay hands on to bless them?
- Find a conference or seminar that offers an impartation service.
- Act as a bridge to give and receive impartations and blessings to other groups in your region.

Further Reading

- *There Is More*, Dr Randy Clark 2013
- *Power of Divine Touch*, Dr. Eva S. Benevento 2016

II

EXPLORING THE GIFTS

5

GIFT OF PROPHECY

Many years ago I was in a men's group that focused on learning to hear God's voice more, first for ourselves, and then for each other. One morning we were ending the group time with prayer for each person present. During the prayer time, we were all praying for my friend. While praying for him, I saw a simple picture in my mind of a mining machine digging out earth, searching for a vein of gold. So I formed a prayer and a simple blessing around that image. I prayed that just as a miner diligently searches for a vein of gold, that he too had been seeking for the Lord, and he surely would find more of God in his life.

After the prayer time, my friend stopped me and said that the picture I used in prayer was exactly the prayer he had been using with the Lord that whole week. He had been praying that he would find a vein of God's glory and presence like a vein of gold is found in a mine. That blew us both away. I saw clearly in an image, what he had been praying in his heart. He was so encouraged to feel that God had seen and heard his prayers.

In essence, I experienced the simple joy of blessing someone through a word of encouragement, or as I Corinthians 14:3 calls them, words of prophecy. In this chapter, we will explore the various ways the Bible illustrates how God speaks to His people. We will expand our expectations of how God might speak to us for our own edification and to encourage and comfort others. We want to encourage the use of the gift of prophecy.

Sometimes when we hear something from God and speak it out, people will affirm that the message is exactly what they needed to hear from God's heart. Sometimes God gives us such an encouraging phrase or timely insight that people around us are blessed. These kinds of utterances do not happen because we think long and hard about what to say or because we considered what the Bible might say about a subject. They seemingly just popped into your head and heart. We say them because these words or images might really encourage someone.

I started to notice this happening more often after I joined a particular men's prayer group. We were intentionally pursuing God's voice and the spiritual gift of prophecy, and we began to hear Him more. It is an amazing thought that God wants to partner with us to speak encouraging or comforting words into other people's lives.

1 Corinthians 12:10 mentions prophecy among the various gifts that are given by the Holy Spirit. Paul says "to another [is given the gift of] prophecy," which is our basis for pursuing prophecy in our churches. But before we get to the gift of prophecy, let us work through what the Bible has to say regarding prophecy in general and hearing God's voice.

God is Always Speaking

When God speaks, we should listen. Every Christ follower asserts this principle is Scriptural. There are simple verses like John 10:27, "My sheep hear my voice," that exemplify this principle. The entire Bible is full of the Father, the Son, and the Holy Spirit speaking. God spoke through the Bible and He is still speaking to us today. Every follower of Christ, even those new in the faith, is able to hear the voice of God.

In the beginning, God spoke and created everything with His words (Genesis 1). In the beginning was the Word, and the Word became flesh (John 1). We have life, not only from food, but by every word that comes from the Father (Mark 11:23). Jesus said we should be hearers and doers of His words (Matthew 7:24-29) and that His sheep hear his voice (John 10:27). The Spirit of Truth, another name for the Holy Spirit, comes to us and speaks (John 16:13), and again the Holy Spirit will speak through us, even as we stand in defense of our Lord. And there are many more examples of God speaking.

There is not enough ink in this book to annotate all the times and places in the Bible that God speaks. Throughout Scripture we are exhorted to listen to the words of the Lord. Here we will focus on the questions that revolve around when God speaks, how He speaks, by whom He speaks, and what He might speak about.

Hearing God's voice, at its most basic, can be broken into two modes:

- Hearing God for yourself - praying then listening for a response
- Hearing God for others and sharing it with them - prophecy

The word "prophecy" means divinely inspired declarations or utterances. To "prophesy" is to communicate such declarations or utterances to others. We all should understand that we can hear God for our own lives, believe we can turn to our loving Father for guidance and hear from Him. We might hear Him through His Word, through a timely sermon, or through His still small voice in our hearts and minds. We hear Him convicting us of sin, giving us peace as we consider difficult decisions, or we may feel a gentle push in our hearts to consider an idea from Him.

So prophecy is hearing God's heart and thoughts for another person or group of people and sharing it with them. In the remaining portion of this chapter, we will look at prophecy through the Bible and learn to understand its place in our own lives and in our churches. First we will examine Old Testament prophecy and when the Spirit of God came upon people. Then we will review Jesus' words regarding prophecy and the role of the Holy Spirit in prophecy. Lastly, we will look at how the early church regarded prophecy and what their expectations were for the use of this spiritual gift n their midst.

As I mentioned, we all should expect to hear God in our own lives. But only a few have an expectation to hear from God concerning others and share it with them. Throughout this chapter our goal is to increase our expectation that God might use any and all of us to prophesy to others. We shall see that the Bible states that we should all prophesy.

Prophecy in the Old Testament

In Luke chapter 7, Jesus spoke of John the Baptist, describing him as a prophet, even the greatest prophet up to that time. But then our Lord Jesus said all who are in the Kingdom of God will be greater than John the Baptist. Jesus challenged us to think of ourselves as capable of being greater than the greatest prophet of the Old Testament. Before we can understand what this really means, we need to look at how God moved among the prophets of the Old Testament and how the Spirit of God came upon them. These descriptions will help establish the standard of what to expect in our lives as we follow Christ today.

The Old Testament is not shy in naming or affixing the term "prophet" to a wide-ranging group of people. Abraham was called a prophet by God (Genesis 20:7), as was Moses (Deuteronomy 34:10). Samuel heard the voice of God at a young age, was Israel's judge and a prophet to kings (Samuel 3:4), Elijah and Elisha had illustrious careers are prophets, as did Jonah, the notoriously reluctant prophet, and the strange prophets Hosea and Ezekiel who seemed to live out prophetic words more often than speak them. Prophets were sometimes also kings, as King David was considered a prophet, as well as farmers, and priests. There were even some with some serious life issues like Hosea with serious marriage issues.

The books of 1 & 2 Kings, 1 & 2 Chronicles, and various prophetic books list many exploits of prophetesses and prophets who proclaimed the word of God to kings, rulers and common people alike. Even in exile, prophets were common in the land of Judah or in cities where the exiled people of Israel had gathered (Daniel and Ezekiel are prime examples).

At various times and places there were also bands or groups of prophets of God. The first band of prophets is seen in Samuel's time. They are mentioned when Saul was anointed king in 1 Samuel 10:10 and again when King Saul was looking for David in 1 Samuel 19:20. Later, during the time of Elijah, a servant of the king protected one hundred prophets in two caves (1 Kings 18:1-15). Again, a group of prophets came to Elisha when Elijah was about to be taken to heaven (2 Kings 2:3-5). That same group is referenced in further stories about Elisha in 2 Kings 4:1, 4:38, 4:42, 5:22 and 6:1.

There are over 130 named prophets in the Bible, sixteen of whom are women, and many more referenced in groups and schools There is very little we could call a common thread that pulls all of these prophets together, except that they were chosen by God to declare His words.

Beyond Prophets Prophesying

Though prophets are common in the Old Testament, many people prophesied even though they were not named prophets. Let's look at what prompted them to prophesy to help us understand prophecy today.

Moses and the Elders

While the people of Israel were traveling out of Egypt, Moses lead them according to the guidance of God. But he become weary and exasperated with the burden of leading the people. So God told him to gather seventy elders, and God would place upon them some of His Spirit to share the load.

> *"Then the Lord came down in the cloud and spoke to [Moses] him, and took some of the Spirit that was on him and put it on the seventy elders.* ***And as soon as the Spirit rested on them, they prophesied.*** *But they did not continue doing it. Now two men remained in the camp, one named Eldad, and the other named Medad, and the Spirit rested on them. They were among those registered, but they had not gone out to the tent, and so they prophesied in the camp. And a young man ran and told Moses, 'Eldad and Medad are prophesying in the camp.' And Joshua the son of Nun, the assistant of Moses from his youth, said, 'My lord Moses, stop them.' But Moses said to him, 'Are you jealous for my sake?* ***Would that all the Lord's people were prophets, that the Lord would put his Spirit on them!'"*** Numbers 11:25-29

In verse 25 we clearly see that when the Spirit of God rested on the elders they immediately started prophesying. Moses does not call the elders prophets just because they prophesied for a time, but he does seem to consider it a good thing if all God's people prophesied.

Saul Among the Prophets

In two stories during Saul's reign, the Spirit of God falls on people and they immediately start prophesying. We mentioned this story in passing already, but here is the full text as the prophet Samuel told Saul what would happen to him:

> ***"'Then the Spirit of the Lord will rush upon you, and you will prophesy with them*** *and be turned into another*

> *man. Now when these signs meet you, do what your hand finds to do, for God is with you. Then go down before me to Gilgal. And behold, I am coming down to you to offer burnt offerings and to sacrifice peace offerings. Seven days you shall wait, until I come to you and show you what you shall do.' When he turned his back to leave Samuel, God gave him another heart. And all these signs came to pass that day. When they came to Gibeah, behold, a group of prophets met him, and* ***the Spirit of God rushed upon him, and he prophesied among them****. And when all who knew him previously saw how he prophesied with the prophets, the people said to one another, 'What has come over the son of Kish? Is Saul also among the prophets?'"* 1 Samuel 10:6–11

The effect of the Spirit falling on Saul was so pronounced that he prophesied alongside the other prophets. We see a similar event take place in 1 Samuel 19.

> *"And it was told Saul, 'Behold, David is at Naioth in Ramah.' Then Saul sent messengers to take David, and when they saw the company of the prophets prophesying, and Samuel standing as head over them,* ***the Spirit of God came upon the messengers of Saul, and they also prophesied****. When it was told Saul, he sent other messengers, and they also prophesied. And Saul sent messengers again the third time, and they also prophesied. Then he himself went to Ramah and came to the great well that is in Secu. And he asked, 'Where are Samuel and David?' And one said, 'Behold, they are at Naioth in Ramah.' And he went there to Naioth in Ramah.* ***And***

> ***the Spirit of God came upon him also, and as he went he prophesied*** *until he came to Naioth in Ramah. And he too stripped off his clothes, and he too prophesied before Samuel and lay naked all that day and all that night. Thus it is said, 'Is Saul also among the prophets?'"*
> *1 Samuel 19:19–24 (emphasis added)*

So powerful is the effect of the Spirit of God coming upon people that three bands of warriors had the Spirit of God descend on them and they all started prophesying. These men were not priests or spiritual leaders. They were soldiers ordered to capture David, yet they started to prophesy when God's Spirit fell on them. King Saul himself pursued David to Naioth until the Spirit of God fell upon him and led him to prophesy as well.

Most of the time when we hear about the Spirit of God falling on people, we think of Samson, Gideon, or other warriors on a mission of God. God's Spirit enables them to do feats of strength, courage, or valor in the midst of hopeless odds. Or we remember times when the Spirit empowered the wisdom of Solomon to guide the nation or Joseph to interpret dreams.

But in these narratives about the elders of Israel and Saul's men, we see that another effect of God's Spirit falling on people is that they start prophesying. This point is very important as we transition to looking at what prophecy looks like in the New Testament. Remember, all of us in Christ have God's Spirit in us. Could what happened to Saul's men happen to us?

Greater than the Prophets

Amos 3:7 asserts that "the Lord God does nothing without revealing his secret to his servants the prophets." If God is still moving in the world, then He still has prophets declaring His thoughts and intentions. But if the Old Testament prophets have finished speaking, who is God's prophetic voice now? The Church is, for we are all greater than John the Baptist, and are full of the Spirit of God!

> *"What then did you go out to see? A prophet? Yes, I tell you, and more than a prophet. This is he of whom it is written, 'Behold, I send my messenger before your face, who will prepare your way before you.' I tell you, among those born of women none is greater than John. Yet the one who is least in the kingdom of God is greater than he." Luke 7:26–28*

Many consider John the Baptist, of whom Jesus speaks in the above passage, as the last of the Old Testament prophets as he declared the coming of Jesus. But the most important aspect of this verse is not naming John as a prophet, but revealing that all in the Kingdom of God, those who believe unto Jesus, are greater than John. Each of us should believe we can be more prophetic than John the Baptist.

Revelation 19:10 states that "...the testimony of Jesus is the spirit of prophecy." John the Baptist proclaimed the coming of Jesus while we proclaim the risen Lord. He was a prophetic voice before Jesus came. Through the Holy Spirit, we have greater prophetic voices proclaiming Jesus in this present day. Our mere testimony of Jesus is prophetic. But there is more than just the testimony of Jesus. Before turning to the specific gift of prophecy, we need to examine what Jesus taught concerning hearing from God.

All Can Hear Jesus & the Father

"My sheep hear my voice, and I know them, and they follow me" (John 10:27). Nowhere in scripture is the "word of God" or "voice of God" ever equated to, or limited to, the written Bible. The Bible is the infallible word of God, sufficient to know salvation in Christ, and for knowing God. It is useful for teaching, training, correcting and rebuking those who have erred (2 Timothy 3:16), and it is the final measure for all actions by individuals and churches in Christ. It is also the standard we test all prophetic words against, since we know the Bible is 100% truth.

But the Bible does not speak into all situations and we do not know God's heart on all matters without constant interaction with Him. Where should I go to minister today? Which city should I live and work in? Should I be a pastor or a business leader? How does God view the person in front of me? How should I minister healing in this situation? Does God have a message for the church in my city? What is God's heart on this matter of politics?

Each of these questions can be answered differently for individual people, and we naturally seek the Lord through prayer for His leading in our unique circumstances. We do this because we can hear the voice of our Shepherd, Jesus Christ, and that our heavenly Father seeks to give us direction in our lives.

Jesus set an example for us in John 5:19 regarding being led by the Father: "Truly, truly, I say to you, the Son can do nothing of his own accord, but only what he sees the Father doing. For whatever the Father does, that the Son does likewise." Similarly, as daughters and sons of the same Father, we can hear and be directed by Him.

Taught by the Holy Spirit

Besides being led by our Heavenly Father, we can hear from and be guided by the Holy Spirit. The Spirit of Truth, another name for the Holy Spirit, was promised and given to each believer in Christ. He dwells with and remains in us. Ephesians 1:13 reminds up that when we believe in Jesus, we are marked with a seal, the Holy Spirit, and He will help teach us and remind us of what Jesus said.

> *"And I will ask the Father, and he will give you another Helper, to be with you forever, even the Spirit of truth, whom the world cannot receive, because it neither sees him nor knows him. You know him, for he dwells with you and will be in you." John 14:16,17*

> *"But the Helper, the Holy Spirit, whom the Father will send in my name, he will teach you all things and bring to your remembrance all that I have said to you." John 14:26*

Some contend that John 14:26 only applies to the twelve apostles, foreshadowing that they will write the New Testament under the inspiration of the Holy Spirit. Such an interpretation is incorrect and is not supported by the surrounding context in

John 14. Also, as we have seen in Part 1, all believers of Jesus Christ receive the Holy Spirit as a seal to our salvation. The John 14 promise fulfills various Old Testament promises that each of us would be taught by the Spirit of God directly.

> *"I will put my law within them, and I will write it on their hearts." Jeremiah 31:33*

> *"And I will put my Spirit within you, and cause you to walk in my statutes and be careful to obey my rules." Ezekiel 36:27*

The Holy Spirit is living inside us not only to teach and guide us but at times to speak through us. In Matthew 10, Jesus declares that the Holy Spirit can and will guide our very words.

> *"When they deliver you over [to the authorities], do not be anxious how you are to speak or what you are to say, for what you are to say will be given to you in that hour. For it is not you who speak, but the Spirit of your Father speaking through you." Matthew 10:19-20*

Jesus said that when persecution comes and we are before rulers and kings, we will speak the words the Spirit gives us. In other words, we will prophesy in front of those leaders. That is what prophecy is: speaking from the power and inspiration of God. This Matthew 10 reference is clearly prophecy.

Finally, in regards to the words of Jesus, the astounding statement that we have already visited numerous times also applies here—"Whoever believes in me will also do the works that I do; and greater works than these will he do, because I am going to the Father" (John 14:12). Jesus was considered a prophet according to the woman at the well (John 4) and the crowds and leaders (Matthew 21:11,46 and John 6:14, 7:40). We should expect to do greater things than He did, including prophesying. Thus we should expect to have in our midst prophets who minister to our cities, families, and businesses.

In the next section, we will show that through Paul's writings, the early churches understood that the Holy Spirit would be moving among them regularly through prophetic utterances.

Prophecy in the Early Churches

The pouring out of the Holy Spirit upon God's people, His church, has had unprecedented effects, especially with respect to prophecy. In Peter's first address at Pentecost, he famously quoted the prophet Joel, stating that as the Spirit rests upon people, they shall start to prophesy, dream, and have visions from God—not as a one time fluke on Pentecost day when the Spirit was given, but an ongoing flow of prophecy from that time forward.

> *"And in the last days it shall be, God declares, that I will pour out my Spirit on all flesh, and your sons and your daughters shall prophesy, and your young men shall see visions, and your old men shall dream dreams..." Acts* 2:17

Prophecy in the Church Age

In our brief review, let us look through the book of Acts and other Epistles to see how the gift of prophecy was used and cultivated in the early churches. Just as there were named prophets in the Old Testament who did not write a word in the Bible, there are many prophets in the New Testament who did not write any of the Bible. In the book of Acts we can find numerous individuals who are named as prophets, yet none of them wrote anything that is in the Bible.

- "Now in these days prophets came down from Jerusalem to Antioch. And one of them named Agabus stood up and foretold by the Spirit that there would be a great famine over all the world (this took place in the days of Claudius)." Acts 11:27-28
- "Now there were in the church at Antioch prophets and teachers, Barnabas, Simeon who was called Niger, Lucius of Cyrene, Manaen a lifelong friend of Herod the tetrarch, and Saul." Acts 13:1
- "And Judas and Silas, who were themselves prophets, encouraged and strengthened the brothers with many words." Acts 15:32
- "And we entered the house of Philip the evangelist, who was one of the seven, and stayed with him. He had four unmarried daughters, who prophesied." Acts 21:8,9

In these verses we hear about Agabus, Judas, Silas, the daughters of Philip, and various people in the church of Antioch all being called prophets. Yet outside of Saul, later named Paul, none of them wrote any passages of the Bible. The reason I am pointing this out is that some groups and churches incorrectly equate prophecy with the Biblical writings and then determine that since the Bible is now complete that prophecy is not needed anymore. The Holy Spirit's inspiration of the Bible is complete, but the Holy Spirit's activity of prompting comforting encouragements and blessings is still ongoing through the gift of prophecy.

Beyond prophets, we later see elders of a church prophesying over Timothy as Paul states 1 Timothy 4:14, "Do not neglect the gift you have, which was given you by prophecy when the council of elders laid their hands on you." When Timothy was commissioned for ministry, the elders spoke prophetic words over him. These elders are not called prophets, but they declared prophetic utterances by the leading of the Holy Spirit.

Prophecy was not restricted to just prophets and elders. Before we get feel comfortable practicing prophecy ourselves, let's review how Paul instructed the early churches concerning this gift.

The Gift of Prophecy

The Apostle Paul is so adamant that the churches should use the gift of prophecy actively that he prefaces many statements with "when you prophesy," not "if you prophesy." Paul's teaching is in line with Peter's understanding that since the Holy Spirit had been given, Jesus' disciples would dream dreams, and speak prophecies (Acts 2:17-21). I Corinthians 11:4-5 corroborates that both men and women prophesied and 1 Corinthians 14:31 insists that "you can all prophesy, one by one." This instruction is an invitation to all churches to allow anyone prompted by the Holy Spirit to prophesy.

Some people prophesy only occasionally, some have the gift of prophecy and exercise it routinely, and some who prophesy are recognized prophets who may have leadership qualifications in the church. But a person with the role of a prophet is not the same as a person with the gift of prophecy. It is clear from 1 Corinthians 14 that prophets and elders are not the only ones prophesying in the church.

In Romans 12:6 Paul says, "having gifts that differ according to the grace given to us, let us use them: if prophecy, in proportion to our faith," and in 1 Corinthians 12:10 says the Holy Spirit gives "to another, prophecy." Paul is clearly instructing members of numerous churches to be active in these gifts, which by extension means our churches and fellowships should encourage the use of the gift of prophecy.

We can now turn to the specifics of the gift of prophecy. Learning to use a spiritual gift or recognize a gift in others is easier when we see it in action in our local church. There should be those called prophets in our midst and there should be people with the spiritual gift of prophecy. Healthy churches should have all the gifts, but prophecy should happen in our corporate meetings as a matter of course. The health and growth of a church is not measured by attendance numbers but by the number of those maturing and operating in their spiritual gifts and callings.

The Greater Gift

Looking at 1 Corinthians 14, the gift of prophecy appears to be elevated over the other spiritual gifts. 1 Corinthians 14:1 encourages believers to, "pursue love, and earnestly desire the spiritual gifts, especially that you may prophesy." Paul highlights prophecy as the gift we should desire the most, explaining that prophecy is higher than the gift of tongues because it can be used to build up the whole church.

> *"The one who speaks in a tongue builds up himself, but the one who prophesies builds up the church. Now I want you all to speak in tongues, but even more to prophesy. The one who prophesies is greater than the one who speaks in tongues, unless someone interprets, so that the church may be built up."* 1 Corinthians 14:4-5

Though Paul elevates the gift of prophecy, that does not diminish the need for the other gifts. A church that is full of only one gift is ill-equipped to build itself up, nor will it be able to fully represent Christ to the world. What Paul is really advocating, is that as you pursue and deepen the gifts you use, also pursue prophecy.

Qualities of Prophecy

In the first few verses of 1 Corinthians 14, God gives us a few measuring sticks to check prophetic words against and confirm that they are from God. Paul told us not to despise prophecy, but to test everything (1 Thessalonians 5:20-21). The four indicators of true prophecy listed in 1 Corinthians 14 are:

1. Must build people up (verse 3)
2. Must bring encouragement (verse 3)
3. Must bring comfort or consolation (verse 3)
4. Must build up the church (verse 4)

Of course not every comforting word or every encouragement is a prophetic utterance. But words that feel prophetic in nature should bring comfort, encouragement, and build people up. If they do, most likely the word was from the Lord. Conversely, if a spoken word tears people down, condemns them, or discourages them, then it is unlikely God was speaking through that person. Such a word was most likely the person's own thoughts or feelings.

Beyond the qualities of bringing comfort, encouragement, or strengthening, we are told to look at the fruit—the results of the prophetic word. Good prophets and prophetic words bring good fruit, and bad prophetic word bring bad fruit (Matthew 7:15-20). Sometimes we cannot instantly understand if a word is from God. But we know a good prophetic word will eventually bear good fruit in the people.

In the same passage that Paul tells us to test prophecies, 1 Thessalonians 5:21 also reminds us to "hold fast what is good". Paul is instructing us not to dwell on things that do not measure up, but to keep close to our hearts all the good prophetic words that are spoken. Critical people and those who are unfamiliar with the big picture of how God works can get hyper-focused on utterances that do not seem to measure up to God's standards. We are not to quench the spirit or sever our partnership with the Holy Spirit and the gift of prophecy, nor to despise or forbid prophecy (1 Thessalonians 5:19-20). Instead we simply to check all prophetic words, and keep the good ones.

We will do well if we keep these guides in front of us. Using these quick guidelines we can start to discern the quality of a prophetic utterance by the Holy Spirit, through the gift of prophecy.

Receiving Prophetic Messages

"I see an eagle flying high in the sky, and the sight of the eagle is so keen that he can pick out a piece of candy corn in a large field. I feel this represents you and how you fly high like an eagle, but also that you can pick out the small details, the important things that really matter." The young lady who gave me this prophetic word did not know me that well, but she was speaking about my spiritual gift of wisdom and was encouraging me to use it whenever I could. My friend received an image God gave her because He wanted to remind me of this spiritual gift. It was timely and encouraging and made me feel the love of God affirming how He made me.

Receiving messages from the Lord is an amazingly large subject on its own. Many good books on prayer and prophecy have been written to help us learn to hear God's voice. He speaks with a myriad of ways and forms. We might hear God during prayer or worship, or while walking in a park. Without trying to be exhaustive, I want to cover a few Biblical ways that God is known to speak.

I will only give one Bible reference, though there are usually many examples for each way of "hearing" from God. Below are examples to help understand how God could use various means to communicate the same idea.[4]

You may receive messages from God when you:

- **See them**: as an internal image in your mind or in a vision (Isaiah 6, a vision of God's throne).

---

[4] This list is expanded from a Global Awakening training, which itself was based on various Vineyard trainings from John Wimber.

Example: You see an eagle in your imagination.

- **Hear them**: as an internal voice that sounds like your own thoughts, in words or descriptions or an audible voice (1 Samuel 3, when the Lord calling to Samuel)
  Example: You hear the words "soaring like an eagle" in your mind.
- **Say them**: in conversation or in prayer, uttering words of revelation that afterwards are confirmed as prophetic (Luke 12:12, the Holy Spirit will give words)
  Example: You say "you are like a soaring eagle" to a friend, and it is the same prophetic word they got an hour ago.
- **Read them**: as words, letters, or numbers in your mind or superimposed over someone or something else (Daniel 5)
  Example: You see the word "eagle" next to someone
- **Dream them**: in symbols and allegorical images and stories that God gives you while sleeping to be recorded and decoded upon waking (Joseph and Daniel were both dreamed dreams and received interpretations)
  Example: The night before a conference you have a vivid dream of eagles flying.
- **Know them**: when a fully formed thought comes into your mind that was not there a moment ago (similar to Luke 12:12, Holy Spirit will give words)
  Example: You just "know" the person has the qualities of an eagle.
- **Feel them**: as if you carry the heart of God over a situation, person, or people
  Example: you feel like the person should be soaring like an eagle.

This list applies not only to prophecy, but also to ways we receive messages for most of the spiritual gifts. These are some of the ways we can learn to hear God speak and deepen our relationship with Him. By being aware of the many ways God might speak, we can better attune our hearts to hear Him in our own lives and for those around us.

A few years ago, a worship leader gave me exactly the same prophetic encouraging word as I just retold, about an eagle flying high and having keen sight. The only change was she said "corn nut" instead of "candy corn." I was blown away that two people who did not know each other at all could give me nearly the same encouraging word years apart. Then eight months later another young lady gave me the same word again! This time, she saw that I was leading a group of eagles. God was expanding the word, for at that time I was entering into a new season of leadership. Paul said all prophecy should be encouraging, comforting, and strengthening (1 Corinthians. 14:3), and accordingly, each time I received this word picture I was greatly encouraged.

If you are pursuing prophecy, be a voice of encouragement in your fellowship or community. You will naturally start to hear the Lord more for yourself. The Apostle Paul felt it was a top priority for the Corinthian church, and by extension our churches, to learn to pursue prophecy. Truly, God wants to invite us to speak encouraging and comforting words into other people's lives. Let us pursue love, and also to prophesy.

Discovering Your Gift

- Do you get images or words in your head that feel like they might encourage someone in a meeting you are a part of?
- Do you dream about people you know, and those dreams give insight, comfort or encouragement for them?
- Do you feel like it is easy to hear from God, both for yourself and others?

Faith in Action

- Ask the Holy Spirit to increase your voice in prophecy.
- In faith, ask to receive pictures, words or insights to encourage a friend and share each with them.
- Join a grace-filled fellowship or group that will allow you to practice and even make mistakes in a safe environment.
- Take an internal survey of your past and determine if have already been used by the Lord to communicate simple prophecies to others that encouraged, built up or comforted them.
- When praying for a person, ask the Lord for words, images or insights that you can communicate to them.
- Take notice if the Lord uses similar words or pictures for you to bless people with. God may be forming a shared language with you to help you hear and see what He is doing.
- See Appendix A, Hearing from God. Prophecy may come in these ways.

Further Reading

- *You May all Prophesy*, by Steve Thompson 2000
- *Approaching the Heart of Prophecy*, by Graham Cooke 2006
- *Prophetic Activation*, by Johnny Eckhedt 2016

6

GIFT OF WISDOM

"That was prophetic!"
"Thanks for that prophetic word."
"You are really gifted in prophecy."
"You should prophesy more."

In many of the churches or fellowships that are opening up to the more of the Holy Spirit, everything is lumped together as prophetic. When spiritual gifts are being explored for the first time or they are re-examined after a period of dormancy in a church, we gravitate toward prophecy or calling everything prophetic. This is natural because Paul told us to pursue the best gift (1 Corinthians 14:1), which is prophecy. Paul's encouragement to prophesy more was not to discourage or disregard the other gifts, but that prophecy can and should be added alongside the other gifts.

But not every activity of the Spirit of God is prophetic. Not every utterance is a prophetic word. Just as the gift of healing is distinct from prophecy, so are utterances of wisdom and knowledge different than spoken prophecies. Just because they all proceed from the mouth does not make them all prophetic. There are various and distinct ways of identifying, sharpening, and practicing the different spiritual gifts.

So we will continue with the study of spiritual gifts. In this chapter we will study another spoken gift of the Holy Spirit, wisdom. Prophecy can be described as saying the things God says. Likewise the gifts of wisdom, knowledge, and discernment can be described as knowing or understanding what God knows. We will spend the rest of this chapter deepening our understanding of what the Bible calls the "utterance of wisdom."

Was it me, or God?

Pride told me I had good intuition. I could get to the core of a matter and give good advice easily. I surprised myself how a picture would come to mind that could quickly explain difficult matters and help a friend make a key decision. I took all the credit for these keen insights or wise words when I should not have.

During my college years, neither I nor the church I was part of had a good understanding of all the gifts of the Spirit. We affirmed them all, but outside of teaching, giving, evangelism, and the service gifts found in Romans 12, the spiritual gifts were not well defined or pursued. Due to my lack of training, I took credit for what the Holy Spirit placed in my heart and mind. In fact, it was an unidentified gift of wisdom active in me.

After a few years and reading the Bible more, I got an inkling that God was dropping into my mind these bits of wisdom. The gift was finally recognized by other groups that were more attuned to the gifts of the Spirit. For many years, I had no understanding of what words of wisdom looked like in practice, which led me to take all the credit and not give God thanks and praise for the timely insights. After I grew in understanding that it was God gifting me these insights, I wanted to be more prepared. I found that much of the time when words of wisdom were being usefully conveyed I was drawing from Scriptural truth. So, I began to saturate my mind with the Bible (especially Proverbs) so that God's truth would be readily available when the Spirit led me.

A young man asked for advice regarding a work matter the other day and a verse from Revelation 2 instantly came to mind. Knowing it was the product of the gift of wisdom, I used the verse to quickly give him wise counsel, and he was very excited about going to work the next day to apply this wisdom. We both praised God for the new direction and insight he had because the gift of wisdom had been active in our midst.

This gift of wisdom is given by the Spirit of God. "For to one is given through the Spirit the utterance of wisdom," 1 Corinthians 12:8. These are specific utterances of wisdom that the Spirit gives to a follower of Christ, which will assist in a specific situation at a specific time. When needed, God, through the Spirit in us, gives an application of wisdom that was not in our minds the moment before.

The Greek word in the verse is 'sophia" meaning "wisdom, broad and full of intelligence." Many times wisdom is summed up in maxims or proverbs but it can also include keen understanding and application of knowledge (Thayer's Greek Lexicon). King Solomon was full of wisdom, and he produced many proverbs (1 Kings 4:31-32), some of which are written down in the Bible in the book of Proverbs. Wisdom can also be applied in management and administration. For example, Daniel, who was taken captive to Babylon, is said to have had much ability in things like scientific understanding, and was gifted as an interpreter of signs and dreams (Daniel 1:17), but he also granted the position as a top administrator of the kingdom.

The best way to consider the gift of wisdom is that it is not spoken out of the accumulated wisdom and experience of a person, but from the wisdom of God through the Holy Spirit. Such remarks could come from a child, an elder, or someone of any age or maturity. God calls us to walk alongside Him as He dispenses wisdom through this gift.

To understand the activity of the gift of wisdom in our lives, we will look at both Old and New Testament for clues. Then we will be able to draw a distinction between general wisdom and the gift of wisdom that comes from the Holy Spirit. Jesus also demonstrated the gift of wisdom, and we will also review how the early church understood and encouraged this gift. But first, let us sharpen our focus by looking at how God depicted the gift of wisdom in the Old Testament.

Wisdom in the Old Testament

Divine wisdom is easiest to find in the Old Testament. The entire book of Proverbs is a compilation of wise sayings given to produce understanding and prudent behavior, and knowing what is right, just, and fair (Proverbs 1:2-3). Proverbs gives us well-rounded examples of what words of wisdom may sound like. But the Book of Proverbs is not the first or only place where wisdom is mentioned. Sometimes we boil wisdom down to pithy quotes, or stories of judges masterfully exposing wrongdoing, like the story of King Solomon exposing the real mother of a disputed child (1 Kings 3:16-28) As a result, the people in verse 28 "feared the king, for they saw that the wisdom of God was in him to administer justice." But wisdom is more than sayings and the administration of justice.

In the Book of Exodus, God instructs Moses to find skilled workmen who shall labor with the spirit of wisdom resting upon them. Exodus 28:3 says, "You shall speak to all the skillful persons whom I have endowed with the **spirit of wisdom.**" This verse connects wisdom to skilled workmanship. Many times wisdom is solely associated with the planning of complicated tasks, judging complicated cases, or establishing a system in society. This verse expands the concept of wisdom to include skilled work with our hands as an expression of wisdom.

Wisdom is also the application of understanding or knowledge. Solomon's courts were marked by amazing administration. In 1 Kings 10, the queen of Sheba speaks of Solomon's wisdom, and describes the works and manner of the servants and their excellence. She noticed that a well-run kingdom was a hallmark of wisdom.

> *"And when the queen of Sheba had seen all the wisdom of Solomon, the house that he had built, the food of his table, the seating of his officials, and the attendance of his servants, their clothing, his cupbearers, and his burnt offerings that he offered at the house of the Lord, there was no more breath in her... Your wisdom and prosperity surpass the report that I heard."* 1 Kings 10: 4-5,7

All of this is because God gave Solomon such "wisdom and understanding beyond measure" (1 Kings 4:29).

Another example of wisdom for ruling a kingdom is found

in the Book of Genesis after Joseph interpreted Pharaoh's dream. God gave Joseph the meaning of two dreams which foreshadowed seven years of great harvest followed by seven years of great famine.

> *"Now therefore let Pharaoh select a discerning and wise man, and set him over the land of Egypt. Let Pharaoh proceed to appoint overseers over the land and take one-fifth of the produce of the land of Egypt during the seven plentiful years. And let them gather all the food of these good years that are coming and store up grain under the authority of Pharaoh for food in the cities, and let them keep it. That food shall be a reserve for the land against the seven years of famine that are to occur in the land of Egypt, so that the land may not perish through the famine." This proposal pleased Pharaoh and all his servants. And Pharaoh said to his servants, "Can we find a man like this, in whom is the Spirit of God?" Then Pharaoh said to Joseph, "Since God has shown you all this, there is none so discerning and wise as you are."*
> Genesis 41:33-39

Joseph proposes a plan to safely navigate the seven years of famine. The court of the Pharaoh recognized the wisdom of the plan and affirmed that God's Spirit was on Joseph. They respected the wisdom flowing from God to Joseph. This wisdom was for the administration of a large social project.

From parables and proverbs to administering justice and kingdom management, wisdom is vital to all realms of life. Reviewing all the instances of wisdom in the Old Testament would take too long. This brief reflection of a few instances of wisdom in the Old Testament reveals that God's Spirit of wisdom was already active in the world.

Wisdom in Jesus' Ministry

All spiritual gifts in the New Testament church find representation in prior ages, for our God does not change. Wisdom is no exception. Jesus moved in wisdom in both His speech and His actions. As Jesus walked the earth, He was our example of holiness and righteousness, and how a human can perfectly partner with the Holy Spirit.

As a youth, Jesus "... increased in wisdom and in stature and in favor with God and man" according to Luke 2:52.The operation of the gift of wisdom in Jesus' ministry is difficult to describe because the Gospels rarely distinguish between the wisdom He grew into and the wisdom that came from the Holy Spirit. Nevertheless, we can be sure that He did minister in wisdom.

First, in Matthew 13, people describe His ministry in a way that should easily be attributed to the work on the Holy Spirit's gifting and power in Him.

> *"Coming to His hometown, He began teaching the people in their synagogue, and they were amazed. 'Where did this man get this wisdom and these miraculous powers?'" Matthew 13:54 (retold in Mark 6:1-4).*

Jesus lived and grew up among them; they did not think his upbringing could have resulted in such wisdom. Their judgement was that His life up to that point could not yield the accumulated experience and wisdom that He displayed. They wondered how He gained this wisdom, but we know it came from God through the Holy Spirit.

In Luke 4:14, Jesus returned from His forty day fast in the wilderness "in the power of the Spirit," but the crowds also attributed to Him wisdom upon His return from that time. The teaching of the Sermon on the Mount astonishes the crowds, "for he was teaching them as one who had authority, and not as their scribes" (Matthew 7:29). Jesus' wisdom was not the wisdom taught by the religious leaders; it was something different. Something directly from God.

Wisdom is not just about making wise judgements. But when it does, it should be mixed with mercy in order to more perfectly resemble the Father's heart of love. In John 8:1-11, we encounter the story where an adulteress is brought before Jesus. The men want to stone her, but Jesus refuses to condemn the women to death. Instead He stoops down and writes in the sand until all the accusers leave. We do not know what He wrote, but surely only wisdom could defuse such a situation.

There are a few more examples of wisdom displayed in the final week before Jesus' crucifixion. The religious leaders were trying to trap Him so they would have a reason to kill Him. They tried to do this without the wisdom of God and were never able to entrap Him.

> *"But, knowing their hypocrisy, he said to them, "Why put me to the test? Bring me a denarius and let me look at it." And they brought one. And he said to them, "Whose likeness and inscription is this?" They said to him, "Caesar's." Jesus said to them, "Render to Caesar the things that are Caesar's, and to God the things that are God's." And they marveled at him." Mark 12:15-17*

Both Matthew 22 and Mark 12 note that after the religious rulers and teachers tried to question him and repeatedly failed to snare Him, they gave up. "After that no one dared to ask him any more questions" (Matthew 22:46 & Mark 12:34). They knew they could not challenge His wisdom.

Jesus spoke with a wisdom that surprised, challenged, and brought mercy and forgiveness to people as well. He is our example. Next we will move to the wisdom found in the early church to complete our study on the gift of wisdom.

Wisdom in the Early Church

The Book of Acts and the Epistles assist us in understanding how spiritual gifts were encouraged in the early churches. Guided by the Holy Spirit, we can grow our faith for the gift of wisdom in our lives by learning how this gift was administered in the first churches.

Wisdom is often paired with other terms in the New Testament: "Wisdom and insight," "wisdom and revelation," "wisdom and understanding," "treasures of wisdom and knowledge" (Ephesians 1:8, Ephesians 1:17, Colossians 1:9, Colossians 2:3). Even though wisdom and knowledge are separate concepts and separate gifts in the Holy Spirit, they are often paired together in New Testament descriptions. Whether in prayers for the churches or through various teachings, the authors of the Bible wanted wisdom and knowledge to abound in the early churches.

In my experience, the gift of wisdom is difficult to recognize as a distinct gift of the Holy Spirit. This gift can hide behind good counseling, wise advice, helpful suggestions, insightful business solutions, administrative structures, and even good church growth strategies.

Wisdom can be hidden in plain sight. A gift of healing or miracles is easily recognized. A word of knowledge that startles someone into saying, "How did you know that?" cannot remain hidden for very long. But timely words of wisdom given in a simple conversation might never be highlighted or noticed in a fellowship as a spiritual gift. As we pursue wisdom, we can also learn to be on the lookout for this spiritual gift in action as well.

However, the early church could tell when the Holy Spirit enabled someone with an utterance of wisdom. In Acts 6:3, the disciples sought out this gift when the first deacons were being chosen: "Therefore, brothers, pick out from among you seven men of good repute, **full of the Spirit and of wisdom**, whom we will appoint to this duty."

Later in Acts 6 the Hellenistic Jews "could not withstand the wisdom and the Spirit with which [Stephen] was speaking" (Acts 6:10). Stephen and Philip were both deacons who were filled with power (Acts 6), but also with spiritual wisdom. This is the first mention of wisdom being associated with an infilling of the Holy Spirit.

Later in Acts 15, we see that the apostles and elders had gathered in Jerusalem to resolve a conflict that had arisen among believers. Some argued that new Christians needed to be circumcised and follow the law of Moses to be saved. On the other side, the apostles Paul and Barnabas disputed this idea. So the Jerusalem elders gathered to resolved this issue. After hearing from the reports from each side and the report from Paul and Barnabas, James spoke:

"It is my judgment, therefore, that we should not make it

> *difficult for the Gentiles who are turning to God. Instead we should write to them, telling them to abstain from food polluted by idols, from sexual immorality, from the meat of strangled animals and from blood." Acts 15:19-20*

The statement, in itself, seems to be a good and wise judgement; an application of wise principles.

But beyond that, the assembled leaders recognized that the wisdom James spoke was greater than his own, as though it were from God. Look at how they worded the letter they wrote to the churches, specifically verse 28: "It **seemed good to the Holy Spirit** and to us not to burden you with anything beyond the following requirements." The counsel gave the exact instructions James suggested and attributed it to the Holy Spirit, not James. They sensed the Holy Spirit in the statement that James presented; this was a word of wisdom in action.

Moving beyond the examples found in the early church in Acts, let us consider the letters written to those churches. The Epistles were written to the churches to help guide and strengthen them. These Epistles have much to reveal to us regarding wisdom in general and the specific gift of wisdom.

1 Corinthians 12:8 "for to one is given through the Spirit the utterance of wisdom" is our foundational passage. The gift of wisdom is *given* by the Holy Spirit. These gifts may be given by the Holy Spirit to any believer. A spirit of wisdom from the Holy Spirit was given to deacons as well as others. Stephen was neither an apostle nor a writer of any book in scripture, yet he had wisdom and the Spirit of God on him. Likewise, we should expect the gift of wisdom in our churches, upon our elders and deacons, and on any that the Holy Spirit chooses.

General Wisdom

Wisdom is such a cornerstone attribute in believers that we see the Father giving us wisdom, the Son giving wisdom, and the Holy Spirit giving wisdom.

The Father gives wisdom

We know we should all pursue wisdom that comes from God. The letter from James explicitly instructs us to ask for wisdom from God: "If any of you lacks wisdom, let him ask God, who gives generously to all without reproach, and it will be given him" (James 1:5).

In Christ, the treasures of wisdom

Colossians tells us that in knowing Christ, we have access to treasures of hidden wisdom: "My goal is that they may be encouraged in heart and united in love, so that they may have the full riches of complete understanding, in order that they may know the mystery of God, namely, Christ, in whom are hidden all the treasures of wisdom and knowledge" (Colossians 2:2-3).

The Holy Spirit gives wisdom

The Holy Spirit wants us operating in His wisdom; it is a gift from Him: "For this reason, since the day we heard about you, we have not stopped praying for you. We continually ask God to fill you with the knowledge of his will through all the wisdom and understanding that the Spirit gives" (Colossians 1:9).

It is amazing that the Father, the Son and Holy Spirit all desire to give us wisdom. From the Father, the Son, and the Holy Spirit, wisdom is given to us. Let us each pursue wisdom from God and recognize those whom the Holy Spirit has gifted with utterances of wisdom.

Sharpening the Gift of Wisdom

We know that all the gifts of the Spirit are given for the common good of the fellowship of believers (1 Corinthians 12:7). Like all the gifts, words of wisdom flow from one believer into the fellowship of believers. This kind of wisdom is not found through extra prayer or deeper study of Scripture. We can all grow in the general wisdom of God, but the gift of wisdom is something different. It is a spontaneous utterance of wisdom, planted by the Holy Spirit into a person, so that the body of Christ can benefit.

Look at Colossians 1:9 again: "Wisdom and understanding that the Spirit gives." This is wisdom given by the Spirit, through the gift of wisdom. If we are not attuned to this gift we could be missing the wisdom God has for our fellowships. If I have a gift of wisdom, and I do not speak with the gift, I could deprive others of godly wisdom and insight that they need. This is why it is so important to use all the gifts God gives. We need each other.

Before leaving the topic of wisdom from the Spirit, let us look at the clearest definition of godly wisdom found in the letter by James, which states, "But the wisdom that comes from heaven is first of all pure; then peace-loving, considerate, submissive, full of mercy and good fruit, impartial and sincere" (James 3:17). This quick study will help us understand when a gift of wisdom is in operation or not. We can measure a spoken word and see if it measures up to the qualities of wisdom with these simple descriptions:

- Is the word **pure** (without taint or stain)? Or does the word feel like it is from the flesh, or colored by the speaker's viewpoint?
- Is the word **peace-loving** (reconciling or uniting)? Or does the word create turmoil and division?
- Is the word **considerate** (thoughtful, fair-minded)? Or does the word only look at one viewpoint, or sound harsh to one group?
- Is the word **submissive** (humble, open-minded)? Or does the word feel like a "my way and there is no other way" command?
- Is the word **full of mercy** (kind,desiring to help)? Or is the word condemning, placing a burden upon the hearers?
- Is the word **full of good fruit**? Does acting on the word bear good results? This test is harder to tell when the word is spoken, but can be discerned over time.
- Is the word **impartial** (not hold favoritism or bias)?
- Is the word **sincere** (authentic, without hypocrisy)? Or does the word feel like a prideful decree?

As each believer and whole fellowships seek words of wisdom together, let us all sharpen our words against Scripture. We should desire our wisdom to drip with the descriptions of James 3:17, whether they come from the gift of wisdom or a measure of the wisdom of maturity and experience.

From the narrative in the Old and New Testaments, we see wisdom is needed in a variety of ways. From governing whole systems of society to making simple life decisions and administering justice to guiding churches through doctrinal issues, wisdom is needed on all occasions. But the Holy Spirit wants to grant us wisdom through the gift of wisdom so we can build up our churches.

As we "follow the way of love and eagerly desire gifts of the Spirit" (1 Corinthians 14:1), let us add utterances of wisdom to our pursuit list. We should desire that all the gifts of the Spirit be strengthened, honored, and released to build up the body of Christ. Let us be the first to stir up words of wisdom to become more active in our fellowships and churches.

Discovering Your Gift

- Do you greatly enjoy the book of Proverbs?
- When you study scripture, does God gives you unique insights?
- When faced with difficulty, do you tend to make wise decisions and choices?

Faith in Action

- Ask the Holy Spirit to increase the gift of wisdom in you.
- Notice when you have spontaneous intuition that helps a friend. This is probably divine wisdom in action.
- Take an internal survey of your past and determine if you have already been used by God with the gift of wisdom.
- When praying for a person, ask the Lord for a verse or a picture in your mind, that will help counsel another.
- See Appendix A, Hearing from God. Words of wisdom may come in these ways.

Further Reading

- *Book of Proverbs*, The Bible
- *God's Wisdom for Navigating Life*, Timothy Keller, 2017

7

WORDS OF KNOWLEDGE

Not too long ago, I was praying for a young lady regarding some family matters. At the end of the prayer, I tacked on a few more phrases I heard in my heart about her young kids being more healthy, and having no more drippy noses in the family. She thanked me for the prayer for her kids because they did have drippy noses that evening. I heard a prayer in my heart and prayed it out loud. It was not anything she asked for, but it was perfectly pertinent to her family. This is an example of a word of knowledge.

In this case, I would not have recognized it as a word of knowledge unless she responded. It seemed like just a tidbit of extra information that popped in my mind about drippy noses that the Lord wanted covered in prayer. I was ready to discount it, but it touched this young mother. This is what being God's hands, feet, and His voice, is all about: timely prayers and encouraging words.

Again, a few years ago, I was on a missions trip to Brazil. Before a service, the group would ask the Lord to reveal any injuries, ailments, or diseases the Lord was indicating He would heal during the next ministry service. While praying, I saw in my mind an image of a man's hand swinging and striking a wall, causing his pinky and ring finger to be painfully swollen. I took a quick note during the prayer time so I would remember this later, and then during ministry time I declared over the microphone that God wanted to heal someone who had struck a wall with their hand and had two small fingers that were badly swollen.

Within five minutes, a young man came to me and explained he had injured his hand exactly as I had described. I prayed for healing in Jesus name a few times, and the Lord immediately healed him. The young man was healed so quickly that he was able to clap his hands together and shake my hand without any pain. Praise Jesus!

At times, God initiates such healings with a word of knowledge to highlight the ailment, disease, or issue He desires to heal. Hearing this revealed knowledge causes faith to grow in the person meant to receive the word because then they know that God "sees" them, and He is concerned with the matters on their heart. In that place of faith, they receive healing in Jesus' name, for "faith comes by hearing" (Romans 10:17). And that is exactly how my story unfolded. It is so good that God allows us to partner with what He is doing through the gift of knowledge.

Wisdom and knowledge are paired together in the Bible often, as they are in Romans 11:33, which exclaims, "Oh, the depth of the riches and wisdom and knowledge of God!" Wisdom and knowledge seem inseparable. But just as we wanted to distinguish prophecy from other gifts, we want to draw a distinction between words of wisdom and words of knowledge.

Though they both come from the same Holy Spirit, they are

listed as separate utterances in 1 Corinthians 12:8: "For to one is given through the Spirit the utterance of wisdom, and to another the utterance of knowledge according to the same Spirit." A word of knowledge by the Spirit of God is to receive a piece of objective knowledge, usually pertaining to an object or something that is factually correct and easily verified. God deposits these facts directly into your mind through His Spirit.

In these verses, the word in Greek is "gnōsis" meaning "knowledge, usually an objective knowledge, or as pertaining to an object" (Thayer's Greek Lexicon). Knowledge here refers to an objectively known piece of information. Practically, a piece of knowledge can be tested with simple "yes" or "no" type questions (this will be illustrated from Scripture shortly).

Through the Spirit in us, God sometimes adds facts of knowledge into our minds that was not there moments before. This is the gift of knowledge in action. A study in the Old and New Testaments will reveal how this gift works and the purposes for which God might use such a gift to bless His people and spread His gospel. As we continue to look at the topics of God-given wisdom, knowledge and discernment, expect God to use you in these ways in your daily life.

Words of Knowledge in the Old Testament

Once again, utterances of knowledge do not come from lived experience or studied knowledge. It is understanding or information you did not have until God gave it to you. Such interactions with God were common for prophets in the Old Testament. In Samuel 9, we see the prophet Samuel meet Saul for the first time.

> *"Saul approached Samuel in the gateway and asked, 'Would you please tell me where the seer's house is?'*
>
> *'I am the seer,' Samuel replied. 'Go up ahead of me to the high place, for today you are to eat with me, and in the morning I will send you on your way and will tell you all that is in your heart. As for the donkeys you lost three days ago, do not worry about them; they have been found.'"* 1 Samuel 9:18–20

How did Samuel know about the donkeys that had been lost for three days? God must have told him. This was a fact that Saul was able to verify and the word of knowledge authenticated Samuel as a prophet. Saul would definitely listen to everything else such a seer of God might say.

Later in Samuel 10, the prophet Samuel gives Saul a long prophetic word describing the events of the next day. Unlike this prophetic word for the future, which could only be verified at a later time, Samuel's words in chapter 9 regarding the donkeys was a word of knowledge. It was factually true at the time when Samuel received it from God and spoke to Saul. It may seem like splitting hairs, but note the distinction in that a future-oriented prophetic word will be true in the future, while a word of knowledge is true in the present. Saul was already looking for donkeys when Samuel shared that fact, and "yes," it was verified later that the donkeys had already been found by Saul's companions (1 Samuel 10:2).

God can reveal minor things like donkeys being found or more consequential intel, like the plans of armies. In II Kings, the prophet Elisha gained a reputation for "knowing" things that he could not have known without spiritual intervention. Even the advisors of neighboring kings knew that God gave

Elisha secret knowledge.

> *"Once when the king of Syria was warring against Israel, he took counsel with his servants, saying, 'At such and such a place shall be my camp.' But the man of God [Elisha] sent word to the king of Israel, 'Beware that you do not pass this place, for the Syrians are going down there.' And the king of Israel sent to the place about which the man of God told him. Thus he used to warn him, so that he saved himself there more than once or twice. And the mind of the king of Syria was greatly troubled because of this thing, and he called his servants and said to them, 'Will you not show me who of us is for the king of Israel?' And one of his servants said, 'None, my lord, O king; but Elisha, the prophet who is in Israel, tells the king of Israel the words that you speak in your bedroom.'" - II Kings 6:8-12*

God was revealing the very battle plans of an enemy king to one of His prophets! The Syrian king thought he had a traitor in his midst because his battle plans kept being revealed to the king of Israel. This was a highly valuable word of knowledge. It saved many lives and perhaps even the entire kingdom.

Here is a modern day story of a general in a third world country who was approached by a man of God. The man of God had received the codes of a battle plan and the general wanted to know how he knew the code words. The man of God explained that God had given him the codes, and that God said the attack would fail horribly if it went forward. Because the man of God knew the codes, the general listened to the rest of the word from God and called off the attack, potentially preventing a devastating war from breaking out. Such is the value of the gift of knowledge.

One last Old Testament example is that of Daniel saving the wise men of Babylon. In Daniel chapter 2, the king demands that his wise men tell him the content of a dream that he dreamed and its meaning and interpretation. How in the natural world are the wise men supposed to know what the king dreamed? The king was testing all of his wise men by asking such a difficult thing. He would not trust the divine interpretation of the dream, unless the person could first describe the dream by way of divine knowledge.

Miraculously, Daniel received the content of the dream through a word of knowledge by God in a vision (Daniel 2:19), and then Daniel was able to interpret the dream by the wisdom of God (Daniel 2:31-45). In this story we see God blessing his servants with knowledge and wisdom. Similarly, as followers of Christ full of the Holy Spirit, we should expect God to bless us with His knowledge and wisdom.

Words of Knowledge in Jesus' Ministry

Moving to the New Testament, we can see how our Lord used the gift of knowledge through the gospel stories. What He modeled is available to us through the same Spirit. Jesus is our example of walking by the power and presence of the Holy Spirit as He interacts with people through words of knowledge on several occasions.

The most straightforward example is found in John 4. Jesus and His disciples were traveling through Samaria and stopped at Sychar, a Samaritan village. As His disciples entered the town to get food, Jesus had a wide-ranging conversation with a Samaritan woman while sitting by a well. They talked about "living water", where worship should take place, and who the Messiah might be. In the midst of this conversation, Jesus tests a piece of information that typifies a word of knowledge.

> *"He told her, 'Go, call your husband and come back.' 'I have no husband,' she replied. Jesus said to her, 'You are right when you say you have no husband. The fact is, you have had five husbands, and the man you now have is not your husband. What you have just said is quite true.' The woman said to him, 'sir, I perceive that you are a prophet.'" John 4:16-19*

Jesus simply knew the fact that she had been married numerous times and her current man was not her husband. The Samaritan woman immediately called Jesus a prophet, acknowledging the supernatural source of that information. However, we are not told how Jesus knew these facts. Was He told by the Father during His walk to the town that He would meet such a woman? Or maybe He received the knowledge in the middle of the conversation? Regardless of the timing, He possessed factual knowledge that He received from God directly. This was a word of knowledge.

Another example of Jesus receiving divine knowledge from the Holy Spirit is in an interaction He had with Peter regarding a temple tax:

> *"After Jesus and his disciples arrived in Capernaum, the collectors of the two-drachma temple tax came to Peter and asked, 'Does not your teacher pay the temple tax?' 'Yes, he does,' he replied. When Peter came into the*

> *house, Jesus was the first to speak. 'What do you think, Simon?' he asked. 'From whom do the kings of the earth collect duty and taxes—from their own children or from others?' 'From others,' Peter answered. 'Then the children are exempt,' Jesus said to him. 'But so that we may not cause offense, go to the lake and throw out your line. Take the first fish you catch; open its mouth and you will find a four-drachma coin. Take it and give it to them for my tax and yours.'"* Matthew 17:24-27

Notice that in the phrase "When Peter came into the house, Jesus was the first to speak" in verse 25, it does not say when "they" entered the house. Peter came in alone, implying that Jesus was in the house during Peter's interaction with the tax collectors. But Jesus seemed fully aware of the conversation, apparently from a word of knowledge from the Holy Spirit. And then Jesus gives Peter a prophetic word to go catch a fish.

Though the Gospels do not describe these interactions as words of knowledge, they clearly depict Christ walking in this gift by the power of the Holy Spirit. Sometimes a word of knowledge is received through a picture or a scene in our minds. Jesus "saw" Nathaniel under a tree before He first met him for the first time.

> *"Jesus answered him, "Before Philip called you, when you were under the fig tree, I saw you." Nathanael answered him, "Rabbi, you are the Son of God! You are the King of Israel!" Jesus answered him, "Because I said to you, 'I saw you under the fig tree,' do you believe? You will see greater things than these.""* John 1:47-50

Like prophetic words, words of knowledge can be received in a variety of ways. You might just know a new fact, or you might see it like Jesus saw Philip. At other times you might hear a sound or a phrase in your mind that gives you the knowledge you need. See Appendix A for a longer explanation of the ways you might receive prophecies and words of knowledge.

Recently, God gave me a word of knowledge that led to a man being healed. During my preparation for a worship gathering, I was asking the Lord to prepare my heart, mind, and spirit to be used by Him. During prayer, I saw a face of a bearded man flash by in my mind. Then I heard the word "fragile" in my head. I did not feel I knew enough, so I prayed again, asking the Lord for more, and I heard this phrase: "Tell him what was fragile is no longer fragile." I try to practice swift obedience, so I made a note to look for a bearded gentleman and pass along this word and see what happens.

After our regular worship service, I approached two men who both had beards. I did not know who to pray for yet, so I casually asked both of them if they had any injuries that would make them feel their body was "fragile." One immediately explained that he had a previous ankle injury, and he walked lightly on his foot because he would frequently turn his ankle. To him it felt "fragile." Through a prayer I declared that his fragile ankle would no longer feel fragile. He did not notice any change at the time, but the next week when I saw him, he told me that his ankle definitely felt stronger. He planted it firmly on the ground a few times in front of me to prove it did not bother him anymore. Praise the Lord!

Words of Knowledge in the Lives of Disciples

The Book of Acts and the other Epistles also describe the spiritual gift of "utterances of knowledge." As with all the gifts mentioned in 1 Corinthians 12, the gift of knowledge was expected to continue to be practiced in all churches. Reviewing how the early disciples used this gift lays a strong foundation for our own expectations today.

It is relatively simple to spot words of knowledge in action if you are looking for them. In Acts chapters 5, 9, and 10, we see three different stories where God gives specific knowledge to his children. This knowledge helped to further His purposes and build faith in His people. Remember, a word of knowledge is a factual, testable piece of information that can be proven true or false.

First, we see a word of knowledge in action when the apostle Peter confronts a couple who lied publicly to the church in Jerusalem:

> *But a man named Ananias, with his wife Sapphira, sold a piece of property, and with his wife's knowledge he kept back for himself some of the proceeds and brought only a part of it and laid it at the apostles' feet. But Peter said, "Ananias, why has Satan filled your heart to lie to the Holy Spirit and to keep back for yourself part of the proceeds of the land? While it remained unsold, did it not remain your own? And after it was sold, was it not at your disposal? Why is it that you have contrived this deed in your heart? You have not lied to man but to God."*
> *Acts 5:1-4*

Though it is not explicitly stated, most commentaries attribute Peter's knowledge of the lie to God giving him that knowledge through revelation. This is a word of knowledge in action. Through this knowledge Peter was able to confront Ananias in his lie. Though this is not a tame narrative since God punishes Ananias and his wife for the lying, it does remind us that nothing is hidden from God. Through the Holy Spirit's gift, members of our fellowships may receive knowledge of things that are hidden in our lives. This is an infrequent but powerful reminder that God does see everything we do.

Now, let's turn to a lighter story, when Saul meets Jesus in a blinding light on the road to Damascus in Acts 9. In this historical story there is another man named Ananias, but he is distinctly different than the Ananias from Acts 5 who died.

> *"In Damascus there was a disciple named Ananias. The Lord called to him in a vision, 'Ananias!' 'Yes, Lord,' he answered. The Lord told him, 'Go to the house of Judas on Straight Street and ask for a man from Tarsus named Saul, for he is praying. In a vision he has seen a man named Ananias come and place his hands on him to restore his sight.'*
>
> *'Lord,' Ananias answered, "I have heard many reports about this man and all the harm he has done to your holy people in Jerusalem. And he has come here with authority from the chief priests to arrest all who call on your name.'*
>
> *But the Lord said to Ananias, 'Go! This man is my chosen instrument to proclaim my name to the Gentiles and their kings and to the people of Israel. I will show him how much he must suffer for my name.'*

> *Then Ananias went to the house and entered it. Placing his hands on Saul, he said, 'Brother Saul, the Lord—Jesus, who appeared to you on the road as you were coming here—has sent me so that you may see again and be filled with the Holy Spirit.' Immediately, something like scales fell from Saul's eyes, and he could see again. He got up and was baptized."* Acts 9:10-18

Firstly, notice that Ananias is named a disciple of Christ. He is not one of the apostles, nor an elder, or a leader in the church of Antioch, but just a disciple. Ananias in this story helps remind us that ordinary disciples can have visions from the Lord (Acts 9:10) receive instruction from Him (Acts 9:11-15) and be used to heal others (Acts 9:17-18). Sometimes spiritual gifts are mistakenly relegated upwards, only into the hands of leaders in our churches. Or worse, it is believed that only the twelve Apostles of the early church were active in such gifts. Part of the ambition of this book is to make it clear that all of the spiritual gifts are still active today in ordinary believer's lives to restore all the spiritual gifts to the whole church in Christ.

One purpose of words of knowledge is to let other people know that God has spoken to you because you know something you should not know. When the Lord tells Ananias that Saul has had a vision, He tells to Ananias a portion of the vision, "In a vision he has seen a man named Ananias come and place his hands on him to restore his sight." Ananias, knowing about the contents of Saul's vision, was authenticated as being sent from God.

A second purpose for words of knowledge is to increase the faith of one or more people. In this instance, because of the word of knowledge, Ananias could come to Saul, a previously dangerous man, see that he had lost his sight, and ask Saul if he had a vision regarding a man coming to heal his lost sight. Once Ananias learned this was all true, his faith for the other parts of the message God gave him could increase; in particular, his faith that Saul was no longer dangerous, that he was God's chosen agent to preach to the Gentiles, and that his sight would be restored through the prayer of Ananias.

In fact, this faith increase usually affects *both* parties involved. Saul had received his own word from God that a man named Ananias would be the one to pray for his sight to return, as seen in verse 12. So both Saul and Ananias would have been very confident that they could trust one another and that Saul's sight would be restored when they encountered each other. This is the second main purpose for words of knowledge; they increase our faith that God is working among us.

Building Faith, Guiding Ministry

Words of knowledge can help us know "who" to minister to, or "how" or "what" should be ministered. In the Acts 9 story above, Ananias learned "how" to minister upon visiting Saul; he prays for Saul's vision to be restored. In Acts 10, we will see how a word of knowledge helped bring together "who" should minister. The whole story is precipitated by God giving specific knowledge to a man named Cornelius so that Peter could preach the gospel to Gentiles.

> *"At Caesarea there was a man named Cornelius, a centurion in what was known as the Italian Regiment. He and all his family were devout and God-fearing; he gave generously to those in need and prayed to God*

> *regularly. One day at about three in the afternoon he had a vision. He distinctly saw an angel of God, who came to him and said, 'Cornelius!'*
>
> *Cornelius stared at him in fear. 'What is it, Lord?' he asked.*
>
> *The angel answered, 'Your prayers and gifts to the poor have come up as a memorial offering before God. Now send men to Joppa to bring back a man named Simon who is called Peter. He is staying with Simon the tanner, whose house is by the sea.'"* Acts 10:1-6

Cornelius, having found favor with God, is told to find Peter and send for him. But beyond the actual command, the angel also passed on factual knowledge of how to find Peter: in the house of Simon the tanner by the sea. Imagine going to the house of Simon the tanner by the sea, and there sits Peter, just like the angel said! These facts guided the search for Peter, but also acted as faith enhancers when they are found out to be true. Finding out you are truly following the steps of God builds faith.

In the story here, the word of knowledge came through an angel, but we know from 1 Corinthians 12 that the Holy Spirit gives this gift to the church, and some people in each fellowship or ministry will be marked by this spiritual gift. Let's expect the Holy Spirit to give words of knowledge in our midst. We can all seek to find those people God who regularly gives words of knowledge and be more faithful and attentive to their words and insights.

I have many friends who are led by words of knowledge from the Holy Spirit. They receive impressions from the Lord such as to go to a mall and share the good news of Christ. Such an impression could feel like a gentle command that should be followed or a picture in your mind that will not go away. Besides the instruction to go to the mall, my friends would often also be given additional information on who to look for while there. Maybe they would be told to look for a college student with a red baseball cap or some other distinguishing piece of clothing or hairstyle. In faith, they would be attentive, knowing they might find a person who is ready to hear God's word. Just like the men Cornelius sent out looking for a house by the sea owned by a tanner named Simon, my friends would be looking to share the loving Gospel of Christ with a person in a mall.

Without a word of knowledge, Ananias might have lacked faith to seek out Saul and heal him in Jesus' name. Without a word of knowledge, Cornelius might not have been able to find Peter, and receive the gospel of Christ. They both decided to enter into an opportunity God was giving them to partner with Him. They were not working for God, they were partnering with Him.

Words of knowledge are one means that God uses to accomplish His purposes, build faith and connect people together and to Himself. They many times can guide us with the "how" to pray or minister just as much as the help us with the "who" and the "what" to minister to. Let us not lose out on all the Holy Spirit want to accomplish in our midst because we did not actively pursue the spirit gift of "utterances of knowledge."

Discovering Your Gift

- Do you get insights about others while praying even though you don't know the person?
- Do you get specific pieces of information that God gives

that could not have been naturally known?
- When you reveal these insights, do people affirm them as correct?

Faith in Action

- Ask the Holy Spirit to increase your word of knowledge gift.
- In faith, ask the Lord for a piece of information that will help cause a breakthrough of God's love.
- Join a small group, or attend a conference that is specifically focused on pursuing spiritual gifts and in particular words of knowledge.
- Take an internal survey of your past and determine if you have already used the gift of knowledge.
- When praying for a person, ask the Lord if there is a specific piece of information that will help the person know they are seen and loved by God (word of knowledge).
- See Appendix A, Hearing from God. Words of knowledge may come through any of these ways.

Further Reading

- *God Secrets: A Life with Words of Knowledge*, by Shawn Bolz, 2017
- *The Spiritual Gifts Handbook*, Randy Clark and Mary Healy, 2018

8

GIFT OF DISCERNMENT

Many years ago I volunteered at an inner city homework center for at risk youth. One of the other volunteers from my church group asked if I knew that a young man had been lying to me earlier that evening. She had witnessed our conversation and seemed to know something I did not. I asked how she knew he was lying: was it the words he used, or had he smirked when he lied? How could I know when I was being lied to in the future? She really could not explain how she knew he was lying. She did not feel anything, but she had a deep knowing that on this occasion the youth was lying.

I went to the youth to find out the truth, and my friend was correct; he admitted to lying. Even more than lying on this one occasion, this particular youth had acquainted himself with a lying spirit. The reason my friend knew this was that she had the gift of discerning spirits. She knew spiritual realities and the presence of spirits, because the Holy Spirit had gifted her with the ability to distinguish between spirits. The verses on spiritual gifts in I Corinthians 12:10 describe discernment as "the ability to distinguish between spirits."

In the last two chapters we focused on words of wisdom and knowledge. Now we are moving to a third type of "knowing" gift called discernment, but this gift is different in a few key ways. Wisdom and knowledge generally happen inside our soul or mind. These facts and insights reside in our minds as provided by the Holy Spirit. But the ability to distinguish between spirits is not necessarily just information or wisdom in our minds; it can come through any of our spiritual senses, like feeling, seeing, hearing, or knowing.

The word "distinguish" between spirits (discernment) from 1 Corinthians 12:10 in the Greek is "diakrisis" meaning "distinguishing, discerning, judging" (Thayer's Greek Lexicon). This judgement is not about passing judgment on opinions or preferences, but as to the correctness of a thing. Applying this "distinguishing" to the spiritual world, the gift of discernment gives the believer the ability to correctly judge the nature of a spirit behind actions, utterances, or presences. Not as a work of judgment or ministry of criticism, the gift of discernment is an invitation by the Holy Spirit to build up the Body of Christ when used well.

The gift of discernment is not a learned skill. It is not heightened perception, hyper-awareness, or mindful attentiveness; it is a spiritual insight. The Holy Spirit gives to some members of the body the ability to know the spiritual backing of attitudes, motivations, actions, and environments. This is the gift of distinguishing between spirits: evil spirits, angelic spirits, the Holy Spirit, or the human spirit. We will use the term "discernment" interchangeably with "distinguishing between spirits" throughout this chapter.

General Discernment

We are all called to grow in our ability to discern between good and evil in Hebrew 5:13-14. "For everyone who lives on milk is unskilled in the word of righteousness, since he is a child. But solid food is for the mature, for those who have their **powers of discernment** trained by constant practice to distinguish good from evil." Hebrews 5:13-14. Distinguishing between good and evil is one hallmark of a mature follower of Christ. Just as our knowledge of Christ should grow, and the wisdom we carry as believers, likewise all maturing disciples of Christ should seek to train their powers of discernment of knowing good from evil. The early church and the New Testament letters that encourage us are full of training, both for general discernment, and also for the gift of discernment.

First, Scripture clarifies the huge difference between the spirit of evil and the Spirit of God (I Corinthians 2:12). Ephesians 2:2 mentions that the spirit of evil (prince of the power of the air) is at work in unbelievers: "following the prince of the power of the air, the spirit that is now at work in the sons of disobedience." Compare that to Romans 8:14: "For all who are being led by the Spirit of God, these are sons of God." The children of God are led by the Spirit of God, the children of the world are led by the spirit of evil.

Secondly, Scripture clearly states that we should test the spirits, which is the activity of general discernment. The gift of discernment comes directly from the Holy Spirit while general discernment is something each of us can train and mature in. 1 John 2 provides a template for testing spirits, and I want to take a look at this passage before we get into the specifics gift of discernment.

Testing Each Spirit

> *"Beloved, do not believe every spirit, but test the spirits to see whether they are from God, for many false prophets have gone out into the world. By this you know the Spirit of God: every spirit that confesses that Jesus Christ has come in the flesh is from God, and every spirit that does not confess Jesus is not from God ... We are from God. Whoever knows God listens to us; whoever is not from God does not listen to us. By this we know the Spirit of truth and the spirit of error."* 1 John 2:1-6

Notice the first exhortation is that we "test the spirits." Every person, preacher, teacher, prophet, or any believer, whether they have a title or not, who says that their words or teaching should be trusted without examination is immediately suspect. We should always be like the Bereans, who examined all of the apostle Paul's teachings (Acts 17:11). The main test is that the teaching or words line up with Scripture and that they have the hallmarks of God's heart.

Next we are supposed to notice if the spirit behind what is being said exalts Jesus as coming from God, not seeing Him as merely a man, a good teacher, or an example of a life well-lived. Jesus was God from the beginning of time. Any spirit that does not confess this central truth is in error at best or a deceiver at worst. And it is not enough to believe that Jesus was God, but that He came in the flesh. Jesus walked as a man, and died as a man. The last check is that they hold the Bible as the final authority in all matters. These tests can be a first line of defense in our spiritual fellowships and churches. We are all expected to operate and grow in this general type of discernment.

Discerning God's Will

Beyond testing the spirits, another fruit of increased discernment is that we can better understand and follow God's will for our lives. We will not be taken astray by the spirit of this world, but we will follow God's path in our lives. Check out these two verses:

- "Do not be conformed to this world, but be transformed by the renewal of your mind, that by testing you may **discern what is the will of God**, what is good and acceptable and perfect." Romans 12:2
- "Walk as children of light (for the fruit of light is found in all that is good and right and true), and try to **discern what is pleasing to the Lord**. Take no part in the unfruitful works of darkness, but instead expose them." Ephesians 5:9–11

In the Romans 12 verse above, we see that most of this discernment is being trained in our minds. Did you notice that before? One great way we can do that is to absorb as much of the Word of God as possible. We should train our analytical processing center in our mind with the truths of God. We should take in inputs, test them, and follow what is judged, or discerned, to be from God. He has a desire that every believer should have a growing measure of discernment to hear, understand, and follow His will in our lives, rejecting the spirits of this world and all their influences.

However, this is not at all the spiritual gift of discernment. Trainable general discernment is different than the gift that is given by the Holy Spirit to certain members of the Body of

Christ, for the common good (1 Corinthians 12:7,10). Instead of connecting to our minds, the gift of discernment, like all spiritual gifts, primarily operates from the spirit of the believer. Just as general wisdom is different than the specific gift of words of wisdom from God, so is general discernment different than the gift of discernment. Take the opening story of this chapter: the things the boy said to me were a lie but they were not the type of thing I could test against Scripture, as he was not talking about Jesus or doctrine, but about his own life, opinions, knowledge, or experiences. The discernment to know he was lying could not be learned.

The gift of discernment is not based on observable data or input, but based on what the Holy Spirit places in the spirit of the gifted person. That knowledge, feeling, or insight is then passed through the believer's mind and conveyed to the rest of the Body of Christ. But the source is not in the mind, but in the spirit of the believer. This is the primary difference between general discernment and the gift of discernment that the Holy Spirit deposits in some parts of the Body of Christ. We will now examine general discernment and the gift of discernment through Biblical narratives.

Discernment in the Old Testament

There is a pronounced difficulty in specifically tracking discerning of spirits in the Old Testament. Many Bible narratives explain which spirits are from God and which from evil. But we, the readers, are not told how it was determined if the spirit was an angel from God or an evil spirit. Still, a few of these stories give us useful hints to the nature of the discernment at work.

In various places in the Old Testament we see angels going

about God's business. It does not take much discernment to distinguish an angel from a demon when the spirit is accomplishing God's purposes. In Daniel 10, it is stated that an angel came to him and explained a vision Daniel had seen. We are also told that angels attended to Elijah (1 Kings 19:5-8), angels of God met Jacob (Genesis 32:1), and an angel closed the mouths of lions for Daniel when he was thrown into the lion's den (Daniel 6:22). These were clearly works of the Lord, and not the enemy.

Other times people were not able to distinguish if a person or spirit was from God or not. When Joshua spoke with the commander of the Lord's army, the angel appeared like a man and Joshua did not know if he was for Israel or there to destroy it (Joshua 5:13-15). Joshua was unable to discern the nature of the angel in front of him. Like all the other gifts of the Holy Spirit, since only very few people in the Old Testament had the Spirit of God on them, they did not all have access to the Holy Spirit to help them discern between spirits. They had to seek out a prophet or seer who would know by the Spirit of God the nature of another spirit.

In the book of Job we read about the interaction between God and Satan. But this information was not available to Job and his friends while he lived through the agony of the devil's work in his life. His friends did not have the discernment to know that this was the work of the devil, and attributed these great problems to Job's presumed sin. Job erroneously blames God for his troubles: "The Lord gave, and the Lord has taken away" (Job 1:21). The entire book of Job seems to have been written as a dialogue between friends with no discernment or idea of what was going on in the spiritual world. What a difference discernment would have made!

But there are a few examples of people who were able to distinguish an evil spirit from other spirits. 1 Samuel 16:14-15 reads, "Now the Spirit of the Lord departed from Saul, and a harmful spirit from the Lord tormented him. And Saul's servants said to him, 'Behold now, a harmful spirit from God is tormenting you.'" In this passage we see that there was some level of discernment among the attendants of Saul, as they could tell when an evil spirit was tormenting him. Sometimes it can be very easy to tell when a spirit is evil versus when it may be good. If the effects of an affliction are severe enough, a gifted person is not needed to discern the nature of the evil spirit.

Many Old Testament prophets chastised the people of Israel because they were not discerning the spirit behind other prophets. Many false prophets would predict peace and prosperity in the land and the people did not test the prophet or the spirit behind the prophet as instructed in Deuteronomy.

- "If prophets or those who divine by dreams appear among you and promise you omens or portents, and the omens or the portents declared by them take place, and they say, "Let us follow other gods" (whom you have not known) "and let us serve them," you must not heed the words of those prophets or those who divine by dreams." Deuteronomy 13:1-3
- "You may say to yourself, 'How can we recognize a word that the LORD has not spoken?' If a prophet speaks in the name of the LORD but the thing does not take place or prove true, it is a word that the LORD has not spoken. The prophet has spoken it presumptuously; do not be frightened by it." Deuteronomy 18:21- 22

Without the aid of the Holy Spirit, the people of Israel could test the spirit of the prophet by checking to see if the prophet tried to entice them away from the true God. Secondly, if what was prophesied did not happen, then it was known that the prophet did not speak by the Spirit of God. This is human discernment, or critical thinking, that we should all seek to possess; to observe and judge a person by the amount of truth their words hold. The people of Israel regularly depended upon general discernment or prophets to help them because there was no Holy Spirit inside them. Conversely, the gift of discernment greatly helps this process of sorting out God from evil. With the Holy Spirit, the Body of Christ can quickly move away from false spirits.

Discernment in Jesus' Ministry

Though examples in the Old Testament are in short supply, the life of Jesus is rich with examples of Him using discernment during His ministry. He is our model to illustrate the cases and circumstances where we too might use Holy Spirit's gift of discernment. We will read a few stories of Jesus in healing and deliverance ministry and the circumstances surrounding these stories.

- "When evening came, many who were demon-possessed were brought to him, and he drove out the spirits with a word and healed all the sick." Matthew 8:16
- "That evening after sunset the people brought to Jesus all the sick and demon-possessed. The whole town gathered at the door, and Jesus healed many who had various diseases. He also drove out many demons." Mark 1:31-33.

- "At sunset, the people brought to Jesus all who had various kinds of sickness, and laying his hands on each one, he healed them. Moreover, demons came out of many people." Luke 4:40
- "In that hour he healed many people of diseases and plagues and evil spirits, and on many who were blind he bestowed sight." Luke 7:31

We can clearly see that during the course of His ministry people brought their sick to Him. He healed some, and cast out demons from others. He discerned which illness was from an evil spirit and which was a bodily ailment or disease. But specifically in Matthew 8, it seems the people already knew who among them were stricken with demons, so it did not take a special gift of discernment for Jesus to minister.

The Luke 4 passage is more generic. The people brought their sick to Him and Jesus healed some and cast demons out of others. He was able to do this because He could distinguish between the human spirit (with its sickly body) from the evil spirits that were afflicting the people. He healed those who were sick and drove out evil spirits from those who were afflicted. The two acts are not interchangeable. Our Lord must have been discerning if the sickness was a physical issue to be healed or an afflicting spirit to be driven away.

Moving on to a new passage, Jesus healed a lame man and the crowd had much unbelief. Jesus could distinguish between His own thoughts and what the Holy Spirit had shown Him where the thoughts of others.

> *And immediately Jesus, perceiving in his spirit that they thus questioned within themselves, said to them, "Why*

> *do you question these things in your hearts? Which is easier, to say to the paralytic, 'Your sins are forgiven,' or to say, 'Rise, take up your bed and walk'?"* Mark 2:8

In this passage discernment almost looks like a word of knowledge. Jesus knew their thoughts, but He perceived it in His spirit. Discernment operates on a spiritual basis while a word of knowledge is concerned with the facts of tangible reality. They may be verbalized in similar ways, but the content is different. My personal experience with highly gifted discerners is that they "feel or know" the spiritual origin of an action or environment from a deep spiritual knowing, and that knowledge does not arise from insight or reflection.

Discernment in Action

One night in a home fellowship, a woman requested prayer for vertigo and dizziness. The pastor sat in front of her and started to pray aloud. The rest of us gathered there also prayed quietly. At the beginning of the prayer time, a young lady came to me with an impression she was discerning that the vertigo was from a spiritual oppression and not just a physical illness. Specifically, she felt that the lady had a cursed piece of jewelry.

If that idea had come straight into her mind stating the lady had a cursed object, then that would have been the gift of the words of knowledge in operation. But in this instance the discerning young lady kept having really negative or agitated feelings about jewelry that were not normal. She knew from experience with the gift of discernment that this indicated some evil spirit attached to some jewelry was in the room. I quietly pulled the pastor aside and communicated what the young lady had told me. With a gentle question, the pastor carefully inquired about if the woman with vertigo had any jewelry that might be involved. The woman responded that she had been given a necklace as a gift by a stranger on the street. She also mentioned that she had received the necklace around the same time the vertigo had started.

The woman went to her purse and pulled out a black medallion with inscriptions that clearly had to do with witchcraft. The pastor asked if the necklace could be thrown out. She gladly destroyed it and threw away the pieces. We prayed more, specifically cancelling any ill effects associated with receiving the necklace or from any spiritual source attached to the necklace. She immediately started to feel better and weeks later was still symptom free. Praise God!

I wanted to share this story because it is a great example of how God could have used a word of knowledge to accomplish the same purpose. God could have told someone with the gift of words of knowledge to ask the lady about the jewelry and the same truth would have been determined. But God used the gift of discernment this time. Either way, the Holy Spirit uses the spiritual gifts for the common good of believers. The lady was set free of spiritual oppression.

Discernment in the Continuing Church

The book of Acts gives a great example of why the gift of discernment is needed beyond general discernment. The apostle Paul's use of this gift will illustrate this difference. In Acts 16, Paul and his traveling companions entered Philippi and remained there for many days. While in Philippi, Paul has an encounter with a spirit of divination in a girl.

> *"As we were going to the place of prayer, we were met by a slave girl who had a spirit of divination and brought her owners much gain by fortune-telling. She followed Paul and us, crying out, 'These men are servants of the Most High God, who proclaim to you the way of salvation.' And this she kept doing for many days. Paul, having become greatly annoyed, turned and said to the spirit, 'I command you in the name of Jesus Christ to come out of her.' And it came out that very hour." Acts 16:16-18*

As we mentioned in the section regarding the Old Testament, the Bible does not usually say how it was known that an evil spirit was present. Similarly it is not said how Paul knew it was a spirit of divination in the girl. But we know it was not general discernment, where one can "use your mind to check the actions of others." How do we know this? Because if Paul had merely listened to the words the girl was saying, that they were servants of the Most High God and proclaiming the way of salvation, Paul would have been excited about how truthful and correct a witness she was giving to them. But instead, Paul was annoyed. This girl was speaking truth but it annoyed Paul because it was coming from a spirit of divination.

Annoyance can be a symptom of the "feeling" or "sensing" type of input that is associated with the gift of distinguishing between spirits, rather than the knowledge or observational approach of general discernment. Many times a signal from a gift of discernment starts with a feeling that something is not as it seems. Paul's mindful analysis could have checked the words of the girl and said, "Yup, she is getting it right," and believed the spirit in her was from God. But instead, he was annoyed. Something in him knew the spirit testifying to him was not from God, and he removed that spirit from his presence by delivering the girl.

Discernment can come from more than just feeling the presence of God or evil. It can be like the gift of prophecy in that the Holy Spirit may speak to our being in various ways of hearing, in visions, or knowing. Discernment can also come from hearing the Holy Spirit speak in your mind about the spirit behind a matter. Other people smell a bad scent when evil spirits are present and good smells when God's Spirit is active; smells that no one else around will smell. It can come from seeing the spiritual world, having a vision of the spirits or seeing them in a dream. Daniel regularly saw and talked with angels and was able to discern that they were angels. Jesus talked to Satan in the wilderness and knew who he was. There are many books written about different aspects of the gift of discernment if you want to pursue a deeper study and others' experience and their growth in the gifting.

Our Lord gave us a very real reason why the gift of discernment is needed in our churches and fellowship in His teachings. Just as the girl with the spirit of divination spoke truth from a wrong source, there will be others who proclaim Jesus but are not known by Him.

> *"Not everyone who says to Me, 'Lord, Lord,' shall enter the kingdom of heaven, but he who does the will of My Father in heaven. Many will say to Me in that day, 'Lord, Lord, have we not prophesied in Your name, cast out demons in Your name, and done many wonders in Your name?' And then I will declare to them, 'I never knew you; depart from Me, you who practice lawlessness!'"*
> *Matthew 7:21-23*

We cannot always judge a person by their words or their actions. Like Jesus described above, the person gifted in distinguishing spirits may help determine the true spirit acting in a person. Sometimes a nudge from the gift of discernment will kick start a group's normal discernment into action. The gifted person will have a feeling that something about a teacher, evangelist, or miracle worker is off. Then, without accusation, others in the Body of Christ can watch a bit more closely and test what is being said and done carefully, or review past actions in a better light.

Many times when people are off, it comes from their human spirit and personal brokenness and not from an evil spirit. The gift of discernment can distinguish between if what is being said or done is from God or one of His angels, evil, or the human. We need to remember there are always three wills at work in everyone's lives: God's, evil, and one's own.

The gift of discernment is not a license to be critical or suspicious. Like all gifts, it is to build up the Body of Christ for the common good. If someone who claims to have this gift is regularly accusing, condemning others, or causing divisions in the Body of Christ, then we should challenge whether they have married love with their gift, or even if they are operating from the Holy Spirit's gift of discernment at all.

> *"And it is my prayer that your love may abound more and more, with knowledge and all discernment, so that you may approve what is excellent, and so be pure and blameless for the day of Christ." Philippians 1:9-10*

Our churches, small groups, and fellowships are not to be in the dark concerning the various spirits in and around our gatherings. Not every spirit, speaker, or visitor is from God and the Holy Spirit. When necessary, believers gifted with discernment can help identify those who have come with a different agenda. The Holy Spirit is constantly inviting us to join in the work of the Father, and through the gift of discernment we can build up the body of Christ. Let us all press in with love, for all gifts are to be wrapped in love, into pursuing more of the ability to distinguish between spirits, which is a gift of the Holy Spirit.

Discovering Your Gift

- Can you tell when someone is insincere?
- Can you sense when situations are spiritually unhealthy?
- At times, can you pinpoint issues or problems before others do?

Faith in Action

- Ask the Holy Spirit to increase your discernment.
- Start noticing rapid changes in your feelings, mood or your understanding of an environment. You might be noticing a spiritual change by the gift of discernment.
- Try and notice if you experience a very quick mood change (positive or negative) when entering a building or encountering a person; you might be discerning a spirit.

Further Reading

- *Seeing the Supernatural: How to Sense, Discern and Battle*, by Jennifer Eivaz, 2017
- *Distinguishing Marks of the work of the Spirit of God*, by Jonathan Edwards, 1741
- *Angels: God's Secret Agents* by Billy Graham, 1975

9

GIFT OF HEALING

Somehow my father contracted kidney disease and his kidneys were shutting down. He needed a kidney transplant pronto or death loomed in the near future. An aggressive steroid treatment was started on the recommendation of doctors, but there were no promises this would work. He took the steroids for several months with no improvement. My mother started telling us to always answer our phones in case we needed to rush to the hospital.

An old family friend who participated in a southern California revival and believed that Lord still heals heard what was happening with my dad. He called my mother to set up a time to pray over him. This man then gathered a few friends and prayed with my father over the phone, praying for healing in Jesus' name. Nothing dramatic was felt during the prayer time, but at the next examination the main kidney infection number started to plummet—a good thing.

It took a couple weeks for his body to come back to full health, but the hard time dealing with a likely fatal kidney disease was ended. The doctor exclaimed that such treatments never bring organs back to their full capacity and never so quickly. But in this case, my father's recovery and the quickness of it was remarkable in the doctor's opinion. We knew it was the prayers not the steroids that brought the healing because the doctor had never seen anything like this happen before.

As in the story in the Introduction, I did not really praise God for His power in healing, but I was very thankful that my father lived. We told others that he made a "remarkable recovery, praise God." We should have praised our God who heals, for He is the Healer, but we did not. I still did not expect God to be the Healer, even though I had a mental theology that said He could heal. It would be a number of years before I started praying for others to be healed and understand that it was part of His name and nature as the Healer.

Physical and emotional healing has been a controversial topic for theologians and ministers of all stripes of Christendom at times. This chapter can in no way summarize the various positions taken by various denominations or groups, but we will attempt to simply let the Scriptures speak for themselves regarding God's actions and intentions regarding healing by His miracle power.

God is the same yesterday, today, and forever. If He reveals His nature in a certain way, that revealed nature remains true for all time. How He shows Himself in the Old Testament will be consistent with how Jesus walked, and it will be in harmony with how the early New Testament churches understood God to act. God has named Himself as "the God who Heals," and that will never cease. As we proceed in this chapter, our appreciation for who God is should grow. Our expectation of knowing and seeing the healing aspect of His nature should grow as well. Our hope is that we all start looking for "the God who heals" to be at work in our churches and fellowships regularly through the spiritual gift of healing.

Healing in the Old Testament

Throughout the Old Testament, we see that God is able and willing to heal among His chosen people and other people groups. God performs healing, describes Himself using healing terms, and promises health and healing in the midst of His people. Throughout the Old Testament, whether it be in the books of the Law, the history books, the Psalms, or the prophets, the name of "the God who heals" is recorded again and again. A review of examples of healing in the Old Testament will quickly establish this point. We will take a little liberty to group them with a thematic approach, adding commentary.

When God describes Himself or gives Himself a name, it is significant. In Exodus 15:26, God connects healing to His character by declaring, "I am the LORD, your healer." Nothing could be more direct than saying that He is a healing God. In this passage the "I AM" construct of God's name links healing to His eternal unchanging nature. God revealed Himself as the great "I AM" to Moses at the burning bush in Exodus 3, and then in this Exodus 15 passage, God expands the I AM revelation to reveal more of Himself.

One of the greatest arguments that enables us to pray for healing today is based on the unchanging nature of how God describes Himself. He is the God who heals. Not a god who once healed in the past. Not a god who may heal in the future. He is the God who heals, in the ever-present moment of "I AM." Let's look at a few of the myriad of examples of His healing nature at work.

Testimonies of Healing

The first recorded healing is found in Genesis 20:17-18, "Then Abraham prayed to God, and God healed Abimelech, and also healed his wife and female slaves so that they bore children." God is directly attributed as the one who healed Abimelech, as well as others in his household to cure barrenness. God is repeatedly shown to be concerned for the barren, opening Sarah's womb in Genesis 21. He also opens Hannah's womb, the mother of Samuel the prophet (1 Samuel 1:9-20). Elisha prayed to God so that a woman could bear children and God answered (2 Kings 4:8-17). Elizabeth's womb was opened and she became the mother of John the Baptist (Luke 1:13-14).

Several books of the Old Testament chronicle the kings and history of Israel; we see God come in healing power to several of the kings. King Hezekiah, during a grave sickness, was told his days had come to an end and that he should place his house in order (2 Kings 20:1-7, 2 Chronicles 32:24-26). That night, he desperately prayed to the Lord God. And God sent the prophet Isaiah to tell the king that God had heard his prayers, and had added 15 years to his life. Hezekiah trusted in God, and his faith was well placed.

In 1 Kings 3, Jeroboam, the first king of northern Israel, sought to seize a prophet of God, and Jeroboam's hand withered when he gave the command. For working against His appointed servant, God wounded Jeroboam's hand. But when Jeroboam cried out, the prophet interceded and the Lord restored his hand. I would never suggest that all illnesses are punishments of God, far from it. But regardless of the origin, calling out to the Lord for healing is a good thing.

King David also knew God as the healing God. David wrote about God who heals (Psalms 30:2, 103:3) and prayed that God would heal him (Psalms 6:2, 41:4). David and the psalmists were well acquainted with the God who heals. Our God is not limited to healing the effects of illness, injury, or disease. He can also raise the dead back to life. Through Elijah the prophet, God raises to life a widow's son. Elijah called upon the Lord, and He listened.

> *"Then he stretched himself upon the child three times and cried to the Lord, "O Lord my God, let this child's life come into him again." And the Lord listened to the voice of Elijah. And the life of the child came into him again, and he revived."* 1 Kings 17:21-22

Similarly, Elisha in 2 Kings 4:18-37 prays to the Lord on behalf of the boy who had died and he comes alive. Following this event, God is known as healer by a foreigner who visits Elisha when ill. In 2 Kings 5 Naaman, an army leader of the Arameans, comes to the prophet to be healed of his leprosy. The king's response shows that the people knew God as the healer, "Am I God, to kill and to make alive, that this man sends word to me to cure a man of his leprosy?" (2 Kings 5:7). The prophet then comes and interacts with Naaman, telling him to dip into the Jordan river seven times to be healed.

> *"So he went down and dipped himself seven times in the Jordan, according to the word of the man of God, and his flesh was restored like the flesh of a little child, and he was clean. Then he returned to the man of God, he and all his company, and he came and stood before him.*

> *And he said, "Behold, I know that there is no God in all the earth but in Israel..."* 2 Kings 5:14-15

Though it was Elisha that directed Naaman to dip in the Jordan, Naaman ascribes the healing to God, not the prophet. God worked through the prophet to accomplish His purposes just as He desires to work through us to accomplish His purposes.

God, Known as the Healer

It is so important that God be known as the healing God that He emphasized it in the promise to return Israel from exile. Jeremiah 33:6 says, "Nevertheless, I will bring health and healing to it; I will heal my people and will let them enjoy abundant peace and security." Even though the context of this passage is the judgment of Israel in exile, along with the promise of eventual return, we can see that the first act of God redeeming His people is to heal them and the land. Before promising to return them to the land, before the promise of peace and security, He promises to heal them.

God expects us to seek Him first in all ways (Matthew 6:33, "seek first the Kingdom," and Proverbs 3:6, "in all ways acknowledge him.") and this includes healing. It is not enough to know that God heals, He actually expects us to seek Him first regarding our illnesses. It is noted in the Bible when King Asa did not seek the Lord regarding a disease in 2 Chronicles 16:12. Also in 1 Kings 1, King Ahaziah was sick and he sent messengers to priests of a foreign god, but the Lord sent Elijah to confront him about not seeking the Lord. God took notice when kings and His people did not turn to Him, for they should have remembered that God is the healing God.

Beyond these specific examples, the Old Testament is replete with passages of the Lord healing and responding to healing prayer. There are examples from Solomon's dedication of the temple to various Psalms (i.e. "who heals all your diseases" Psalms 103:3) and Proverbs mentioning healing through God's hand, and the many promises of God to heal in the books of the prophets. The Lord our God is revealed as the healing God throughout the Old Testament. God's nature is consistent in the work and life of His Son, Jesus as well.

Jesus, The Healer

Not many who call Him Lord and Savior have ever disputed that Jesus healed. All four gospels are packed with stories of Jesus healing; from healings He initiated (the pool of Bethesda in John 5), to healing intrusions while He teaching (paralytic man through a roof in Luke 5:17-39), healing across vast distances (Centurion's servant in Matthew 8), or healing someone right next to Him without initiating it (the woman with the issue of blood in Luke 8:43-48). Numerous times He healed ALL who came to Him (Matthew 4:23, 9:35, 12:15, 14:34-36, Luke 4:40, 6:17-19 & 9:11).

Some of us have adopted complex theologies surmising why some people do not get healed. But in the ministry of Jesus, who only did what He saw the Father doing, He healed all who came to Him. He was showing the nature of the Father as Healer.

Many commentaries rightly point out that these works point to the divine nature Jesus carried while here on earth. When He healed a paralytic man (Luke 5:17-39), He noted that He had the authority to heal and to forgive sins, which the leaders of the day attributed to God alone. The religious leaders were offended that Jesus implied his own equality with God, but the common people were amazed and glorified God for healings that they saw.

Similarly, when John the Baptist was in prison, he sought to know for sure if Jesus was the Messiah. Jesus did not answer directly, but pointed to His actions and miracles to authenticate His message and mission. He cites His ministry of healing as proof that He carried the enduring attributes of God the Father, the healing God.

> *''And when the men had come to him, they said, "John the Baptist has sent us to you, saying, 'Are you the one who is to come, or shall we look for another?'" In that hour he healed many people of diseases and plagues and evil spirits, and on many who were blind, he bestowed sight. And he answered them, "Go and tell John what you have seen and heard: the blind receive their sight, the lame walk, lepers are cleansed, and the deaf hear, the dead are raised up, and the poor have good news preached to them."'' Luke 7:20-22 ESV.*

Though the healings Jesus performed pointed to His Deity, they are more than a pointer. They were the demonstration of an ongoing promise and the nature of God from both the Old and New Testament. The Almighty God, the God who Heals, does not just do enough miracles to authenticate that Jesus was God. He continues to exhibit His nature throughout time.

Healing in the cross

The prophecies in Isaiah 53 regarding the Messiah are clear about how He would suffer and die for our sins and transgressions. "But he was pierced for our transgressions; he was crushed for our iniquities; upon him was the chastisement that brought us peace, and with his wounds we are healed" (Isaiah 53:5). Even though He was sinless, He would bear our sins and make us righteous. But the end of verse five clearly states "and with his wounds we are healed."

Matthew 8 demonstrates we should take this promise of healing seriously and literally. The chapter begins with two specific narrations of Jesus healing people. First, the healing of a leper, and then of the great faith of the Centurion for the healing of his servant. Immediately after those two healings, Matthew notes a vast set of healings: "That evening they brought to him many who were oppressed by demons, and he cast out the spirits with a word and healed all who were sick. This was to fulfill what was spoken by the prophet Isaiah: 'He took our illnesses and bore our diseases'" (Matthew 8:16-17). Verse 17 directly quotes Isaiah 53:4, "Surely he took up our pain and bore our suffering, yet we considered him punished by God, stricken by him, and afflicted." These verses directly link the outpouring of healing in Jesus' ministry to the Isaiah 53:4-5 verses, which promises that we can have an expectation of healing based on what Jesus did on the cross.

The healings of Jesus do not only point to His divinity, but link the eternal nature of God, the One Who Heals, to the loving God who forgives our sins through the sacrifice of Jesus. Our justification from sin was fully paid for and our spirits made completely new and alive on the day of our salvation.

But salvation works its full effect over time, which is the sanctification process. (Philippians 2:12). And healing in our bodies and souls is a part of this sanctification process. We are not instantly healed in mind, body, and soul the day we are saved. Instead there is a process of seeking God to meet us in our dysfunctional brokenness as our Healer and deal with these areas.

It is the will of God that we be healed. It is the desire of God that we prosper in health in our body and soul, so much so that Jesus was wounded and died for us (III John 1:2 and 1 Thessalonians 5:23). He paid so much for our salvation and healing. Later, we will see in James that the church is given a protocol to pray for the sick. The expectation is that God wants all to be healed and to come to Him first for that healing. We do not need a complex theology for why God does not heal. We do not need to hold onto our illnesses to make us "better people" or sanctify us. The Father desires that all be saved and all be healed; so much so, that Jesus suffered. It is our individual and corporate faith and expectation that needs to change, not the nature of God.

Healing and Forgiveness Flow From the Cross

It cannot be stated enough times: if we believe, through saving faith, that our sins will be forgiven when we trust in Jesus, likewise we should believe through sanctifying faith that our sicknesses will be healed through the same work on the cross. Peter says this exact thing, as he encouraged the churches in 1 Peter 2:24, "He himself bore our sins in his body on the tree, that we might die to sin and live to righteousness. By his wounds you have been healed."

In many places, I have noted that we do not necessarily need to change our theology, but change our expectations. Most of us know God healed in the Old Testament and that Jesus healed, too. But we should expect Jesus to heal us today. How and when He chooses to heal us may seem mysterious at times (as part of our working out our salvation) but we should still expect God to heal. We should go to Him first with our diseases and sicknesses. In the next section, we will investigate how and when the disciples expected healing through the name of Jesus.

The Disciples Healing in Jesus' Name

The key to our living for Christ rests in what the Bible says regarding our ordinary everyday lives. If the immediate generation of disciples after the original Apostles had certain expectations or practices in the Lord, we should have similar exceptions and practices. Our foundation for this is found in Jesus' words in Matthew 28:20, "... teaching them to obey all that I have commanded you ...". If Jesus told the original twelve disciples to do anything, then those commands were to be passed to each generation of disciples, and those instructions were to be lived out daily.

The expectation for healing in the name of Jesus is firmly built upon the foundation of God's name as Healer and the ongoing promises of healing through His work on the cross. We will now build on that foundation a practiced healing theology flowing from what Jesus commanded His disciples to do from what the early church leaders taught. My journey into the things of the Holy Spirit started a few years ago in 2011, but it was not until early 2014 that I really started to seek God as the healing God. I devoured books, watched videos, and went on a ministry trip, all seeking God more on this topic of healing in Jesus' name.

On the bus ride from the airport to the first missions outreach, the bus coordinator challenged us to raise our expectations of what God might do. In my prayer time, I took this to heart and asked God to see something I had not seen before, to see a deformed foot or clubfoot straighten.

To my amazement, a couple on the team was ministering a few days later to a young mother whose son had a badly deformed foot. He was carried most of the time and could not run. Through the power of Jesus' love and the ministry of the Holy Spirit, the foot straightened during prayer. First a little bit, and then more and more until it was straight. The boy's mother started crying and sobbing as the little boy started walking in front of her and doing little skips. I caught it all on a video with my phone, and I definitely expect God to do it again and again.

Initial commands and promises

Jesus repeatedly instructed His disciples to heal by His power. First, He instructed the twelve disciples in Matthew 10:7-8, "And proclaim as you go, saying, 'The kingdom of heaven is at hand.' Heal the sick, raise the dead, cleanse lepers, cast out demons." This event is also captured in Luke 9:1. Later Jesus expands this commission to 72 disciples: "After this the Lord appointed seventy-two others and sent them on ahead of him, two by two, into every town and place where he himself was about to go... "Heal the sick in it and say to them, 'The kingdom of God has come near to you.'"" (Luke 10:1,9).

Beyond these commands, Jesus promised that all His disciples would do greater things than He did. John 14:12 says,

"Truly, truly, I say to you, whoever believes in me will also do the works that I do; and greater works than these will he do, because I am going to the Father." Earlier we listed a small portion of the healings that our Lord did, and He placed an expectation on us that we will do even more than He did. Combining the idea that we can heal in His name and that we shall do greater works than He did will spur us forward to accomplish His healing purposes today.

Finally in Mark's version of this commission, we see a promise to all who believe in Him, "they will lay their hands on the sick, and they will recover" (Mark 16:18). Such promises should expand our expectations, but beyond these promises, we can see the church disciples living out these promises to heal in the name of Jesus.

Healing as They Went

The book of Acts starts very abruptly. Jesus ascends to heaven, the Holy Spirit descends upon the faithful in the upper room, followed by the first-ever sermon proclaiming Jesus as Lord and Savior, which results in thousands coming into the Kingdom of God (a quick summary of Acts 1 & 2). In the very next chapter, we read about the everyday lifestyle of disciples gathering to the temple for teaching and worship.

> *"Now Peter and John were going up to the temple at the hour of prayer, the ninth hour. And a man lame from birth was being carried, whom they laid daily at the gate of the temple that is called the Beautiful Gate to ask alms of those entering the temple. Seeing Peter and John about to go into the temple, he asked to receive*

> *alms. And Peter directed his gaze at him, as did John, and said, "Look at us." And he fixed his attention on them, expecting to receive something from them. But Peter said, "I have no silver and gold, but what I do have I give to you. In the name of Jesus Christ of Nazareth, rise up and walk!" And he took him by the right hand and raised him up, and immediately his feet and ankles were made strong." Acts 3:1–7*

This healing in Jesus' name allows a second opportunity for Peter to present salvation through Jesus Christ. Peter was not on some special assignment or missionary journey. He was not led by God to that man. He was just walking to the temple, and God used him to heal a lame man.

Later, God used Peter so mightily in healing that people lined up on the streets so that his shadow might pass over them to heal (Acts 5:15–16). Paul, the most prolific author of the New Testament, was also used greatly in healing miracles. It was noted that handkerchiefs that he blessed would be carried to the sick and they would be made well (Acts 19:12). Peter and Paul simply carried the power of God that was resident in them.

Not Only for the Apostles

Healing by the Spirit of God is not solely in the domain of the early apostles or only for the writers of the Bible. Some have argued that just as healings prove Jesus as Divine, healings authenticate the portions of Scripture written by the apostles. This line of thinking does not hold for two reasons. First, Jesus' healings flowed from His nature and the work at the Cross. Secondly, numerous New Testament authors were not named apostles and had no healings or miracles attributed to them, including Luke the gospel writer, Jude, and James.

Conversely, there are many people in Acts who heal or perform miracles in Jesus name who never wrote a word of the New Testament. "Many who were paralyzed or lame were healed" (Acts 8:70) by Philip the evangelist. Ananias healed Paul's blindness through the power of God. And there was a group of disciples who prayed for boldness and acts of healing, "And now, Lord, look upon their threats and grant to your servants to continue to speak your word with all boldness, while you stretch out your hand to heal, and signs and wonders are performed through the name of your holy servant Jesus." (Acts 4:29-30). Stephen performed many miracles in Jerusalem which led to his martyrdom (Acts 6:8-15). Barnabas (alongside Paul) worked many signs and wonders in Iconium (Acts 14:3).

Between these examples of non-Apostle disciples who performed miracles and healings without writing any Scripture and Scripture writers who did not appear to perform any miracles or healings, we should put to rest the idea that healing in Jesus' name was reserved for only the early Apostles or Scripture writers. God's Word is clear that healing in Jesus name is available to every disciple of Christ, throughout all times.

Healings Authenticate the Gospel

Still, some want to persist in the idea that healing in the name and authority of Jesus is not to be pursued as a regular expression by believers. Some teach that Paul proclaimed the Gospel and demonstrated it with healings and miracles, which was a one-time authentication of the gospel message. This line of thinking holds that once the gospel was authenticated initially, no other signs or wonders were needed. But this does not make sense for either Paul's mission or in the churches he continues to write to.

God worked miracles through Paul to authenticate his message to each city, not to validate Paul as worthy to write Biblical letters. He was not even planning to write the letters when he was planting churches and performing miracles in Jesus' name. The miracles authenticated the gospel he was preaching. In his own words, "For I decided to know nothing among you except Jesus Christ and him crucified. And I was with you in weakness and in fear and much trembling, and my speech and my message were not in plausible words of wisdom, but in demonstration of the Spirit and of power" (1 Corinthians 2:2-4).

On the nature of the kingdom of God, Paul writes that it "does not consist in talk but in power," (1 Corinthians 4:20). The kingdom is established not with a one-time demonstration of power to be talked about in the future, but a continuing presence of power in action. Likewise, we proclaim the gospel with words, but also to display it at work with demonstrations of power.

Healing in Churches

We have already covered the passage in 1 Peter 2:24 where he exhorts us to expect healing and forgiveness because of what Jesus did on the cross. Peter's healing message was directed to a church full of disciples, not unbelievers. This is important because at times 'healing evangelists' have popularized the idea that healing should only be associated with the proclamation of the gospel. But such an idea is not consistent with Scripture. In James 5, there is another exhortation of healing in the church with practical guidelines:

> *"Is anyone among you sick? Let him call for the elders of the church, and let them pray over him, anointing him with oil in the name of the Lord. And the prayer of faith will save the one who is sick, and the Lord will raise him up. And if he has committed sins, he will be forgiven. Therefore, confess your sins to one another and pray for one another, that you may be healed. The prayer of a righteous person has great power as it is working."* *James 5:14–17*

James outlines what should be a regular practice in all churches for all disciples—seeking prayer on behalf of the sick. The confession of sins and an expectation that they "may be healed" are included. Sick people are not comforted and told to persevere. They were encouraged to seek prayer for healing as an ordinary part of church life.

Specifically Equipped to Heal

All of these Biblical narratives demonstrate that the churches the apostles encouraged through letters were planted with an expectation of healing in Jesus' name. They were established amid signs and healings. They were taught to continue to exercise the gifts of the Spirit, which included healing and miracles.

Beyond the general exhortations to expect healing, Paul writes in 1 Corinthians that the Holy Spirit uniquely equips some for this work. All of 1 Corinthians 12 is dedicated to gifts that the Holy Spirit distributes to the churches, and verse 9 specifically mentions healing: "to another gifts of healing by the one Spirit." Having spent this entire chapter building up the expectation that God still heals today through Jesus' name, it is encouraging to know that the Holy Spirit equips the church to fulfill God's purposes today. The spiritual gift of healing is the power of the Holy Spirit which regularly works through the gifted member to accomplish healing in the physical body.

Notice the plural "gifts" of healing in I Corinthians 12:9. There can be a variety of gifts of this type, not just one single way the Holy Spirit works healing through a person. Beyond an understanding of healing in Jesus' name or the empowerment of elders to pray for the sick, the Holy Spirit gives certain disciples of Christ a special grace to effect healings through Jesus' name.

Like all gifts, the gift of healing is something the Holy Spirit works through us. Just as we cannot prophesy whenever we want, a disciple with the gift of healing cannot heal every time they lay hands on people. Just as a person with a prophetic gift does not speak for God every time they open their mouth, likewise the healing gift does not effect healing simply because they pray. But many times such a person with a healing gift will see people healed at a higher rate than the rest of thc church or fellowship, and they will be drawn to praying for the sick.

All of the particulars on how to administer healing gifts and how to sharpen a healing gift are outside the scope of this chapter. We also will not cover what to do when someone is not healed. There are many great books and seminars specifically targeted at building faith and practice around the gift of healing. The only way to know if you have a gift of healing is to start to try to heal the sick or injured through the power of Jesus.

From the Old Testament to the ministry of Christ through the establishment of the earliest churches, God has been ministering healing. I hope that this chapter has sparked the hope and desire for the gifts of healing that are available through the Holy Spirit, and that it would be present and active in our fellowships and churches. And if it is not present, I pray that God will dispense more of this gift upon your church.

Our expectations change when our understanding of who He is and what His ways are start to match what is shown in His word. The Bible states that we worship and serve a healing God. Our Lord healed while He ministered here on earth, and there is healing through the Holy Spirit even to this day through prayer and the gift of healing. Our God is still demonstrating that He is "the God who heals" today.

Discovering Your Gift

- Do you look for opportunities to pray for the sick?
- Do you desire to pray for miraculous healing often?
- Has God used you to bring healing to those who are sick?

Faith in Action

- Approach your elders and leaders to pray for you when sick, and expect to be healed
- Visit ministries or locations where healing in Jesus name is a regular activity.
- Go on a missions or a ministry trip where healing is an expected expression of demonstrating the Gospel of Christ.
- Pray and seek to know the God Who Heals.

- Ask God to reveal the spiritual root of any mental or physical issue you can't seem to shake off.
- Do you have any lingering or untreated pain? Take a moment to address any infirmities with prayer and take them to "God our healer."

Further Reading

- *Authority to Heal*, Ken Blue 1987
- *Power to Heal*, Randy Clark 2015
- *Walking in Supernatural Healing Power*, Chris Gore 2013

10

FAITH AND MIRACLES

Earlier I shared about a college party that was interrupted by the bad news of a father dying in the hospital. I shared how a bold prayer bubbled in my heart and I prayed that the man would be healed, and that he would be healed so fully that he would be discharged from the hospital the next day. Praise the Lord, it happened just as I prayed.

Upon reflection I know this prayer was an instance of the gift of faith. I had such a certainty of the specifics of what I should pray. In faith, I did not believe he would *eventually* be healed; I felt led to add a specific and short time frame to my prayer. I had a sense of clarity, a sense of assuredness, that the prayer I prayed was not just a good prayer, but was exactly what would happen.

To this day, I rarely have had such surety in a prayer as I did that night. It was a gift of faith in action. When a person is so sure of a thing that after praying there is a certainty it would happen, this is the gift of faith. The gift of healing is obvious when it is in operation and when it is not. The spiritual gifts of faith and miracles are also noticeable when they are active.

Some choose not to pursue these gifts because when God does not show up it can be disheartening for the person who thought God was going to move. But that should not deter us. The Holy Spirit wants all fellowships of Christ to be fully active in all the spiritual gifts, including faith and miracles. Paul claims these as spiritual gifts: "to another faith by the same Spirit, to another gifts of healing by the one Spirit, to another the working of miracles" (1 Corinthians 12:9-10).

In earlier chapters regarding the power of God, we have already investigated miracles in a general sense. Miracles are by definition acts of supernatural power. A demonstration of God's power results in a miracle. Or said another way, miracles are the intersection between the normal flow of nature and the power of God. Many Christians believe in miracles to some degree, so I will not belabor that point. The gift of miracles would simply be a gift deposited by the Holy Spirit, enabling a person to conduct miracles as led by the Holy Spirit.

Miracles and faith tend to work together, so we are addressing both in this same chapter. While miracles are a visible sign, faith is a spiritual gift that affects the heart of a believer, enabling them to trust something will come to pass.

Faith

The spiritual gift of faith can be given a simple definition, but is harder to speak about since faith is such an integral part of our lives as disciples. We are going to spend a bit of time on general faith and then explain how the spiritual gift of faith is different. Then we will come back to how the gifts of faith, miracles, and healings intersect.

To get a grasp on the gift of faith, we must start with a working definition of faith. Gladly, the Bible gives us exactly that in Hebrews 11.

> *"Now faith is the assurance of things hoped for, the conviction of things not seen. For by it the people of old received their commendation. By faith we understand that the universe was created by the word of God, so that what is seen was not made out of things that are visible."*
> *Hebrews 11:1–3*

Faith is an assurance, a conviction, pointing at something that is beyond you. Faith is the substance that moves us to reach out into the unseen. Convictions are something you hold firm, even something you fight for. Faith gives us a conviction for things that are beyond what we can see, feel or touch.

Immediately faith is illustrated in verse 3. An example of faith that is common to most Christians is the understanding that something cannot come from nothing, and therefore God must have created the universe by invisible means. This faith in creation rests in our minds. We believe it to be true. But most faith is not expressed through rationalization, but through action. Faith leads to conviction, and conviction leads to action. James so clearly states this: "show me your faith apart from your works, and I will show you my faith by my works" (James 2:18).

In the chapters regarding the gift of wisdom and the gift of discernment, we realized the qualities and characteristics we have as followers of Christ are different than spiritual gifts in action. Though there is a gift of discernment, Hebrews 5 exhorts us all to train our ability to discern good from evil.

Also, there is a spiritual gift of wisdom that is different than the timely general wisdom we can ask of God according to James 1. But nowhere is this more important than concerning the spiritual gift of faith. We are all to live a regular life of faith in Jesus. There are two kinds of faith all believers have: saving faith and ongoing faith. Once we look at these two faiths we can correctly know when a spiritual gift of faith is in operation.

First and foremost, faith is a gift from God. Jesus is the "founder and perfecter of our faith" (Hebrews 12:2). Ephesians 2:8 says, "for by grace you have been saved through faith. And this is not your own doing; it is the gift of God." In other words, Jesus enables our faith, and faith saves us: believing faith for salvation is that gift—so we are saved by grace.

Beyond this initial faith by which we are saved, we are called to have an ongoing faith in Christ. 2 Corinthians 5:7 says that we walk by faith. We are made spiritually alive through our faith, and then we continue to live each day by faith. Galatians 2:20 also reminds us that we have ongoing life through faith in Christ, "And the life I now live in the flesh I **live by faith** in the Son of God, who loved me and gave himself for me." Our Christian life is sustained through faith in the Son of God. So we see that all of us have faith for salvation and for daily life. But this faith is different than the spiritual gift of faith that the Holy Spirit may deposit in a member of the body of Christ.

Nearly all the spiritual gifts are supposed to be normal parts of a growing disciple's life. All are told to pray for the sick, and all are told to grow in discernment, but that does not mean we all have the gift of healing or the gift of discernment. Similarly, we should grow in faith and have it build up in us. Acts 16:5 states, "so the churches were strengthened in the faith, and they increased in numbers daily." If the early churches were strengthened in faith, so should we. Jude 1:20 reminds us we can build ourselves up in faith. Though we all should grow in our faith in God, not all of us have the gift of faith.

A spiritual gift takes a new believer further in the acts of healing, discernment, or faith than other followers of Christ, who may take years to master a discipline they do not have a gifting in. One with a gift of healing may see many people healed, whereas someone else may pray for healings for years and only see a few. The gift of faith may enable someone with the gift to have extraordinary trust or a knowing of what to pray that is beyond what they have cultivated in their personal time with God. It is simply a gift from the Holy Spirit.

Other books have been written on how we actually receive the faith to believe in Jesus for salvation and I am not trying to add to those tomes. Nor will we seek to develop disciplines to grow our faith each and every day, though that is a very worthwhile endeavor. We are going to sharpen our focus on how we might understand and develop the spiritual gifts of faith in 1 Corinthians 12:9 along with the gift of miracles.

To distinguish general faith from the gift of faith, I want to borrow a definition from Sam Storms, who gives this succinct definition for the gift of faith:

> *"The gift of faith is that mysterious surge of confidence which rises within a person in a particular situation of need or challenge and gives an extraordinary certainty and assurance that* ***God is about to act*** *through a word or an action."* The Beginner's Guide to Spiritual Gifts, *Sam Storms*

The main emphasis in this definition is the timeliness of

assurance that this faith brings. The gift of faith is not faith in the general character of God, nor a response of faith to a promised truth in the Bible. It is a surge of faith for a particular time and place, for a particular need.

Acts Faith in the Old Testament

Hebrews 11 is called the "hall of fame" of Old Testament faith. Through its brief summaries of faith, a picture emerges of what comprises acts of faith. When God wanted us to understand faith, He spent only a few verses describing faith, then spent a whole section illustrating faith through actions. Like many concepts, it is easier to understand through example than mere definition, so this section will include examples.

Without trying to draw deep lessons of faith from the lives of these men and women, we can glean a few aspects of what faith in action looks like. This will help us recognize when a gift of faith is active in our fellowships. Consider the summaries of Hebrews 11 as an invitation to go back into the Old Testament and read the whole story.

In Hebrews 11:4-6, the narratives of Abel and Enoch are recounted. Abel brought acceptable sacrifices, and Enoch pleased God because he had faith that God rewards those who seek Him. Both Abel and Enoch sought to worship God, and God blessed their faith. Those who seek Him are commended. And faith always results in a belief-to-action sequence. When you believe something, it results in action. Enoch and Abel believed God rewards those who seek Him, so they were determined to seek Him and worship Him.

The rest of Hebrews 11 gives us examples of faith that move from general lives of worship and faith (Abel and Enoch) to specific instances of faith. Verse 7 notes that Noah responded to God's warning by building an ark. His faith enabled unmistakable action: the construction of a very large boat. Faith enables you to build a boat in a land where there is no water in sight and where it has never rained. Faith always leads to action, however illogical those actions may seem to others.

Verses 8 through 19 speak of the faith of Abraham and Sarah. They believed God and took action by leaving their known home region to venture into a foreign land even when they were not told where they were going. Again by faith, they believed for a son even in their old age. Logic says that a barren woman that is ninety and a man that is one hundred cannot start a family. But they believed in the faithfulness of God to fulfill His promise of a child even when it seemed naturally impossible. Faith does not appear after a promise is fulfilled by God, it comes before it.

Isaac and Jacob had such faith in what God had showed them that they pronounced detailed testable blessings upon their children. Joseph was so sure God would bring the people of Israel out of Egypt that he made his sons swear to take his body with them and bury him in the land of Canaan when they left Egypt. Even though these men never saw the fulfillment of their faith, their faith moved them to issue public blessings and proclamations that were recorded in the Bible for eternity. Sometimes faith in God will lead you to proclaim something far-reaching or profound.

Further in Hebrews 11 we read that Moses' parents disobeyed a direct order of the Pharaoh and baby Moses' life was spared. Under Moses' leadership, by faith the people of Israel entered the Red Sea and walked on dry land as the water parted. By faith an army walked around a walled city, and the walls fell. A flurry of activities and miracles are attributed to faith, including those "who through faith conquered kingdoms, enforced justice, obtained promises, stopped the mouths of lions, quenched the power of fire, escaped the edge of the sword, were made strong out of weakness, became mighty in war, [and] put foreign armies to flight" (Hebrews 11:33-34). None of these triumphs occurred with mere belief, but with earnest effort and actions propelled by faith in God and His promises.

Many consider this James 2:18 verse controversial: "show me your faith apart from your works, and I will show you my faith by my works." But this analysis is confirmed and fleshed out by Hebrews 11. Faith builds trust that can be acted upon. Faith drove men and women of God to act throughout the Bible. Faith is not a meditative construct to contemplate or ponder. Faith is the substance that drives men and women into action.

Faith Leads to Miracles

My point is not to establish that all these stories are examples of the gift of faith, but to show what acts of faith looked like in the Old Testament. Looking deeper at a few examples in the Old Testament, we can directly tie to faith and miracles together. Often, an act of obedience stemming from faith becomes the springboard to a miracle. We will explore this connection between faith and miracles a bit more.

I want to highlight a repeated sequence that we see throughout the Hebrew 11 examples and elsewhere in Scripture. First God, or a prophetic voice for Him, gives an insight, promise, or command. Second, one or more people respond in faith that leads to specific actions. Third, a miracle results from the faith-filled actions that is beyond what would be expected in the natural world. This faith-action-miracle sequence is repeated throughout the Bible.

Moses performed many miracles by faith during the exodus from Egypt and to overcome many trials in the wilderness. Each time Moses pronounced a judgment or plagues against Pharaoh and the people of Egypt in Exodus 6-13, it was an act of faith. Moses could not make even one of these plagues happen but he pronounced them in faith and each one happened. Each time he heard from God, his act of faith was in repeating the words of God (or prophesying) in public before Pharaoh and his whole court. Pronouncing that an event will occur ahead of time is an act of great faith.

Marching around a walled and fortified city for seven days is in itself an act of faith, which resulted in another miracle. Stone walls, multiple feet thick, plastered together do not fall down simply because a large group of people shout and blast horns. God moving in power alongside His people is why the walls fell down. In Joshua 6, the Lord instructs the army of Israel to walk around the city for seven days. With a shout, the walls fell down. There was no natural reason a loud shout would cause the walls of a city to crumble. Sometimes faith leads to illogical actions that allow us to see Him move in a miraculous way.

Acts of faith can never produce the effect of a miracle by themselves. If this were possible, we could work at manufacturing miracles all the time. But acts of faith are a way for us to join in with God's intentions. He invites us into the story of His miracles by asking us to add our faith before He moves. The army walking around a city does not cause walls to fall. But the faith exhibited by the army obeying the words of God released the miracle God had in store.

In 2 Kings 4 we read the story of a container of oil that poured out more than it could hold naturally. In this historical account, a widow is about to lose her children to a creditor, and she asks the prophet Elisha for help.

> *"And Elisha said to her, 'What shall I do for you? Tell me; what have you in the house?' And she said, 'Your servant has nothing in the house except a jar of oil.' Then he said, 'Go outside, borrow vessels from all your neighbors, empty vessels and not too few. Then go in and shut the door behind yourself and your sons and pour into all these vessels. And when one is full, set it aside.' So she went from him and shut the door behind herself and her sons. And as she poured, they brought the vessels to her" (2 Kings 4:2–5).*

The widow is in financial need, but Elisha does not give her money. He does not ask God to create a stack of coins. Instead, God directs Elisha and sends the widow on a journey of faith and obedience. At that moment, she could have resigned herself to losing her children and not followed Elisha's instructions. Or she could act in faith, gather many vessels as the prophet said, tip over her oil jar, and start filling the jars. Her faith was shown by gathering the vessels and pouring. The miracle then occurred inside the activity of her faith. The miracle does not occur without the actions resulting from faith.

We could go through every book of the Bible showing this pattern. God has still interacts with this dynamic of acts of faith resulting in miracles. This is also exactly how Jesus ministered. Moving to the Gospels, we will explore the connection between faith and miracles.

Faith and Miracles in Jesus' Ministry

It is difficult for us to relate with how Jesus lived on earth. He lived so perfectly by faith because He was so connected to the Father that he did what the Father was doing and spoke what the Father was speaking. It is easier to relate to the disciples and the people who came to Jesus in need of a miracle or healing.

First, let's focus on the miracles. Our faith increases when we remember what God has already done. Similarly, recounting a few of the miracles of Jesus and His disciples helps us recognize the gift of miracles active in our churches, home groups, and fellowships.

The Miracles of Jesus

Outside of the resurrection, the only other miracle mentioned in all four gospels is the feeding of the 5000 men, which would have also included uncounted women and children (Matthew 14:13-21, Mark 6:30-44, Luke 9:10-17, and John 6:1-14). In this famous miracle, Jesus takes five loaves of bread and two fish, and miraculously multiplies it to feed all the people present. The powerful hand of God to multiply food is, of course, a miracle.

In the Gospel of John, John repeatedly speaks of the signs Jesus performed. Signs are just another way to describe a miracle. The first sign Jesus performed was turning water into wine found in John 2:1-12. Jesus has lists of miracles: He walked on water (John 6:16-21), raised three people from the dead (Lazarus in John 11; daughter of Jarius in Mark 5; son of a widow in Luke 7), fed 4000 at another time, and He calmed a stormy sea (Luke 8:22–25; Matthew 8:23–27; Mark 4:36–41).

Each of these signs is a miracle performed by Jesus, a list that does not include all the healings and breaking of demonic powers that were regular occurrences in His ministry. It would be impossible to write down all of Jesus' wonderful works (John 21:25).

Christ's ministry was marked with miracles and He said we would do greater things than He did (John 14:12). Through the Holy Spirit, the gift of miracles has been distributed to the body of Christ, allowing us to do miracles as Jesus did.

Faith for Miracles in Jesus' Ministry

Connecting miracles, healings, and faith is not difficult when reviewing the works of Christ. If miracles are bursts of supernatural power from a source outside the natural order, via God, then to believe for a miracle before it happens is an act of faith—a conviction of things unseen (Hebrews 11:1).

Let us look at a situation where the faith and the miracles that Jesus worked are linked: "[Jesus] could not do any miracles there, except lay his hands on a few sick people and heal them. He was amazed at their lack of faith" (Mark 6:5-6). Here in Mark 6:5, Mark categorizes healing as a type of miracle. A miracle is simply an outpouring of God's power. Restoring blind eyes, giving strength to lame men, and curing leprosy are all displays of God's power.

Second, this passage tells us that little or no faith results in few or no miracles. Another example of little faith resulting in no power for miracles is when the disciples could not cast out a demon. They went to Jesus for answers about why the display of power did not happen. Jesus replied, "Because of your little faith" (Matthew 17:19-20).

Let me take a moment to make sure you do not hear something I am not saying. Many healings and miracles are *not* connected to the faith of *the person in need*. In the verses above, Jesus was addressing the disciples about their faith, not the faith of the demonized boy. There are many examples where the sick or demonized do not have faith and are still healed. Lazarus was raised from the dead in John 11, and he obviously did not possess any faith for his own resurrection. His sisters had faith in the resurrection at the end of times, but lacked faith that Lazarus could be made alive at that time, and yet Jesus still worked the miracle.

John 5:1-9 recounts the story of the man Jesus healed by the pool of Bethesda. The man also seemed to lack faith, yet Jesus healed him. Likewise, when Jesus calmed the storm, He chastised the disciples for their lack of faith, yet he worked a miracle in their midst to stop the storm. God can and does providentially heal and perform miracles without us and our faith. But is also clear that a lack of faith disables our ability to partner with God in what He is doing. A lack of faith can interfere with the flow of healing and miracles. We do not want Jesus to be amazed at the "lack of faith" in our churches like He was in Mark 6:6. We need to allow the flow of the Holy Spirit in the gift of faith, miracles, and healing in our churches. This flow is not about working harder in the spirit, but having the mindset that God wants to heal and work miracles in and around our churches, through each of us.

With faith present, Jesus moved mightily. Earlier we made the connection that faith prompts action in a person. In many of these Bible narratives where people are healed, the faith of the person caused them to approach Jesus and ask Him to help them. These people believed in Him enough to seek Him out and make a request of Him, usually for healing or freedom from demonic oppression. It takes faith to ask for a miracle. There are many Biblical accounts that could be studied at a deeper level to discover more connections between how faith and healing miracles interact. Here are some highlights of people seeking out Jesus in faith:

- The Centurion asked Jesus to heal his servant (Matthew 8:1-13)
- Jesus saw their faith and healed a lame man (Matthew 9:1-9)
- A woman touched His cloak and was healed (Matthew 9:18-26, Mark 5:34)
- Jesus healed two blind men and a mute who had faith (Matthew 9:27-33, Mark 2:5)
- Jesus healed the daughter of a Canaanite woman (Matthew 15:21-28, Mark 7:24)
- Blind Bartimaeus had his sight restored (Mark 10:46-52)
- 10 lepers were healed (Luke 17:11-19)
- A blind beggar was healed (Luke 18:35-43)

In each of these instances, Jesus credited the faith of the person as He heals them. When we come to Him believing He can accomplish what we ask, that is a huge display of faith. Faith is an important ingredient for miracles and healings in Jesus' name.

Gift of Faith in Action

Reviewing how Jesus administered healings and miracles only gets us part of the way to understanding how faith, healing, and miracles work together. We still need to discuss how we might know when the Holy Spirit is working in us or others around us in a gift of faith. Let me share another story that illustrates faith and healing together.

During the mission trip to Honduras I mentioned earlier, I had another encounter with the gift of faith. But this time I easily recognized it as the gift of faith because I had taken the time to study the gifts. In this situation I had a real time epiphany, "This is the gift of faith!"

We were out doing street evangelism and inviting people to the night service at a nearby church. I was in a group of some young men and women and a translator talking to people about their need for Jesus. We prayed with any who wanted to accept prayer in Jesus' name. One lady led us to her apartment building and said we should pray for people in a certain apartment. She led us up a stairwell to the second door down the hall.

The lady knocked on the door and shouted something through the window. A few moments later the door opened slightly. There was hardly any light in the home so I could not make out any features of the person who opened the door. In that moment, I had this huge surge in my chest. It was like a balloon rapidly inflating in me spiritually and emotionally. The figure at the door had not spoken a word yet, but I absolutely knew that they were going to be healed in Jesus' name. Such an intense certainty rushed over me that if they had known English I would have probably started praying for them without any further introduction.

As it was, the person at the door was a young lady. I knew culturally it would be inappropriate for me to pray for her directly, but the faith in me was so strong I knew I did not have to do the praying. I let the young women on my team pray. But this faith made it so I knew the result would be a healing in Jesus' name. After a short set of prayers, that is exactly what happened. The young Honduran women had had an intense pain in her side for days, and during the prayer in Jesus' name, the pain vanished miraculously. The certainty of that particular outcome was the gift of faith in action for this situation and time.

I believe that at times, we lack the faith to seek or declare a purpose of God, but through the Holy Spirit, God gives us a gift of faith to push us over the top into action. There are times when we might be too timid to boldly pray for healing, but the gift of faith infuses us. We start to believe for the impossible and that spurs us to take actions we may not normally take.

An instance of the gift of faith is recognizable and verifiable because what was prayed about or commanded happens. On this trip I heard a leader tell a story about when a lady was healed of blindness. He had been ministering healing prayer for some time with no breakthrough. Then he was led by God to question the blind woman regarding the circumstances of the sudden onset of blindness. During the questioning, he felt God pinpointed how to pray for the woman. At the moment he received the insight, he said he felt such a confidence of faith rise up in him that he told the woman and her surrounding family that he was going to pray one more time, and this time she was going to receive her sight. After praying multiple times and not seeing anything change, it takes a lot of faith to declare that God is going to do a miracle.

He was so sure that he practically guaranteed the woman that she would no longer be blind after he prayed (something he would normally never do and would never counsel a prayer team member to do). He then prayed in Jesus' name according to the insight and surge of faith God had given him, and she immediately received full sight in both eyes.

The minister explains that this faith was not drummed up from inside himself. It was given to him by God, by the Holy Spirit through the gift of faith, and this led to action and a healing miracle. This gift of faith from the Holy Spirit raised his faith, but it also affected the faith of the family and of the blind lady. They all saw the miracle that God intended as sight was restored to a blind person.

Faith and Miracles in the Early Church

Faith and miracles were constantly part of Jesus' ministry. But identifying the Holy Spirit's gift of faith and miracles is a little harder. Thankfully, the acts of the apostles and the early churches are full of instances of these gifts in use.

God used Peter to heal the lame man outside the temple in Acts chapter 3. Earlier we looked at this story from the perspective of the gift of healing. Here we will look at Peter's testimony of the event, which suggests that a gift of faith was involved, too. As Peter and John were nearing the temple, they passed a man who had never walked and was known as the beggar by the Beautiful Gate. The man asked Peter for money, but instead Peter healed the man in Jesus' name. This healing caused an uproar in the temple area and Peter was able to preach salvation through Jesus. In his sermon he speaks of the faith in Jesus' name, as well as a faith that is through Jesus.

> *"And his name—by faith in his name—has made this man strong whom you see and know, and the faith that is through Jesus has given the man this perfect health in the presence of you all." Acts 3:16*

The portion that reads "faith that is through Jesus" implies that Peter received a faith directly from God for this particular miracle. He received a gift of faith that resulted in his bold declaration to the man to get up and walk. Very early after the Holy Spirit was given, Peter is already exhibiting the gift of faith and healing in action.

Further on in the life of the early churches, Paul addresses the gift of faith when writing the Corinthian church. In 1 Corinthians 12-14, the discourse on spiritual gifts and of love, Paul gives an example of the gift of faith. He is describing the use of spiritual gifts without love, but the example lets us see the gift of faith in action. 1 Corinthians 13:2 reads, "and if I have all faith, so as to remove mountains, but have not love, I am nothing." Paul implies that a gift of faith will result in a miracle: moving a mountain. A gift of faith is almost always connected to healings, miracles, or other bold actions like moving entire mountains. Second, we see that it is entirely possible to operate in a gift of faith and still lack love. We should not operate this way, but imperfect people, unloving at times, can still have faith that flows from the gift of faith and work amazing miracles and healings.

Writing to another church in Galatia, Paul mentioned the Holy Spirit's activity among them. Galatians 3:5 states, "does he who supplies the Spirit to you and works miracles among you do so by works of the law, or by hearing with faith ..." We established in an earlier chapter that this passage points out that God continued to move mightily in this church even after the apostles left the region. These powerful works of God, these miracles were the spiritual gift of miracles in action. The verses state that God supplied the Spirit and that Spirit worked miracles among them.

While miracles almost always require faith, the gift of faith can appear without a notable miracle as a result. Sometimes the gift of faith leads to ordinary-seeming actions and outcomes. The gift of faith may be stirred up in a particular situation to have a bold trust in God. There are instances of a gift of faith being the catalyst for a missionary to start an orphanage, adopt a child, move to a foreign land, or stop and evangelize because the outcome feels assured. None of these things seem like miracles, but they can be a result of a gift of faith.

Faith is Not Presumption

Neither the gift of faith, nor the gift of miracles, operate in presumption. They do not function by praying and declaring that God is going to move in this way or that way. They are not gifts where we start testing God by running your car past empty and believing in God for another measure of gasoline. God may use a person, giving them faith for a miracle at times, but that does not mean they can pull on God "in faith" to make anything happen that they desire.

Like all spiritual gifts, the gift of faith and the gift of miracles are not something the person who is gifted can just "use." They are still gifts of the Spirit, guided and directed by Him. But when we know He uses us or others in these ways, we will be more expectant and attuned to partner with what He is doing through us to bless the community. A spiritual gift does give us license to assume God will move the way we desire, rather, the gift of faith aligns us with God's desire, which often surpasses our own. God guides and directs us, not the other way around.

But at the same time, we do need to take risks. If we believe we are in a situation where the gift of faith is activated in us, we need to take bold action. We need to pray for the sick and step out. We may need to make bold proclamations if we know that is what God is calling for in that situation. We need to be aware of when the Holy Spirit is moving and be looking to identify the gift of faith or miracles in others and in ourselves.

Pressing in For More

Like all spiritual gifts, acknowledging that the Holy Spirit can and should be moving in our midst with gifts of faith and miracles is the main step toward seeing an increase of these gifts in our churches and fellowships. Creating an expectation and providing space for God to move in both faith and miracles will lead to an increased measure of the gifts. We can only fan into flames the gifts that we know we have (2 Timothy 1:6). And we can only encourage others in gifts we know they have.

Honoring instances of these spiritual gifts in use helps the whole church be more attentive to how the Spirit of God moves with these gifts. As we desire and pursue all gifts (1 Corinthians 12:31, 1 Corinthians 14:1), we must also pursue the gifts of faith and miracles, and honor them among the other gifts.

I once heard it said that a church could go years without needing a healing or miracle, but if the gifts of giving and administration disappear, the church could dwindle and die in no time. But I do not think that is true. Such churches might seem to function well with attendance, offerings, and seeing the community impacted with the love of God, but without the dynamic power of the Holy Spirit moving in faith, healings, and miracles, such fellowships are incomplete. According to the pictures of the early churches found in the Book of Acts and the other Epistles, all the gifts are needed and should be in operation to have a spiritually healthy church, which cannot be measured according to worldly markers like attendance numbers or giving amounts. To become Biblical churches that are fully spiritually alive, we must honor and use the gifts of faith and miracles.

Discovering Your Gift

- Do you believe God will use you to enact His miracles?
- Does asking God for big things excite you?
- Do miracles often happen when you are nearby?
- Have you had surges of confidence in knowing God's intention, and you pray boldly in that confidence?
- Do you have a constant desire to see God's miraculous power?

Faith in Action

- Notice if you or anyone in your fellowship swells up in faith when faced with an insurmountable obstacle.
- Notice if an expansion of faith rises in you when requested to pray for a sick person or asking God to solve an impossible problem.
- Visit a fellowship or ministry that believes for and sees miracles happen in their ministry or outreach.
- Without getting into theological arguments, visit a Word of

Faith group to experience their mindset towards walking in faith.

Further Reading

- *True Stories of the Miracles of Azusa Street and Beyond*, Tommy Welchel 2013
- *Miracles: The Credibility of the New Testament Accounts*, Keener, Craig S. 2011
- *When Heaven Invades Earth*, Bill Johnson 2013

11

TONGUES AND INTERPRETATIONS

In my college days, my friends and I had spirited discussions on theology and Scripture. We definitely had conversations about the gifts of tongues and the interpretation of tongues. These spiritual gifts were not practiced or recognized in our church; they were a mystery. Most of the time I wondered what the practical use of such spiritual gifts could be when we had bilingual members who could translate a pastor's message into Spanish or Chinese as needed.

Some taught that tongues and interpretation were the accelerated ability to learn a new language for missionary work. The implication was that if you were not a missionary, you did not need to pay attention to this gift at all. This line of thinking always seemed like a strange conclusion about a spiritual gift that was supposed to build up the whole church, not just missionaries. I was always intrigued by stories about the use of tongues, and these stories expanded my thinking. Unfortunately, in those years I never received solid teaching on the spiritual gift of tongues.

I still remember an interesting story a friend told me about the gift of tongues. He had gone away to a southern California Christian college. They had a guest speaker come and the whole college attended his seminar. My friend was seated next to an Asian student that had difficulty keeping up with the large fancy words the speaker was using. To help him, my friend started leaning over and paraphrasing the talk into simple English.

The Asian exchange student seemed to appreciate the help and stayed engaged the entire time. At the conclusion of the seminar, the Asian student turned to my friend and asked him when he had learned Chinese. My friend replied that he did not know Chinese. My friend spoke in English, but the other student insisted everything my friend said was in his native dialect of Chinese.

The interesting thing about this story is that I am not sure if my friend was speaking in a language he did not know without realizing it or if the Asian student experienced a miracle of interpretation, wherein he heard Chinese while my friend spoke English. I am not sure to this day, but one way or another, the student was built up. It was definitely accomplished by the gift of tongues or interpretation, as enabled by the Holy Spirit.

It is similar to the Biblical narrative of the day of Pentecost when the disciples left the upper room after receiving the Holy Spirit and spoke to the Jewish crowds from around the world, who "were bewildered, because each one was hearing them speak in his own language" (Acts 2:6). The spiritual gift of tongues and interpretation is listed in I Corinthians 12:

> *"To each is given the manifestation of the Spirit for the common good. ... to another various kinds of tongues, to another the interpretation of tongues."* 1 Corinthians 12:7, 10

The word for "tongues" in the original text is the Greek word, "glossa." Glossa can mean either "an organ of speech" or "a language" (Vine's Expository Dictionary of New Testament). The context of 1 Corinthians 12:10 implies the second meaning; languages, not physical tongues in mouths. The Greek idea is similar to the English phrase, "mother tongue," being the language of the culture or nation a person grew up speaking. By these two gifts, the Holy Spirit enables people to speak a certain or distinct language and at times the Holy Spirit enables an interpretation of a language.

According to the Oxford dictionary, a language is "the method of human communication, either spoken or written, consisting of the use of words in a structured and conventional way." The two main points to take away from this definition is that languages are structured, and their primary function is to communicate or express the thoughts or feelings from one person to another. One function of the spiritual gifts of tongues and interpretation is to help communication inside the body of Christ. All the gifts are given for the common good (1 Corinthians 12:7), and a diverse body of Christ might fragment if language barriers are not torn down. Galatians 3:28 reminds us that "There is neither Jew nor Greek ... you are all one in Christ Jesus," but if we cannot speak to one another, true unity is quite difficult.

Tongues in the Old Testament

At the Tower of Babel, God confused the language of all people, and the people scattered across the world (Genesis 11). Now God is gathering a people called through Jesus, our Lord and Savior, into unity and oneness as the Church. In the gathering of the church in a region, the Holy Spirit enables unity by breaking down divisions based on language. The Holy Spirit breaks down walls that might prevent the gospel of Jesus from being preached to other peoples and nations. Isaiah 49:6 reminds us God is too zealous to stop at saving just one nation: "I [God] will make you [Israel] as a light for the nations, that my salvation may reach to the end of the earth."

The Old Testament does not have many examples of tongues or the interpretation of tongues as enabled by the Holy Spirit, unlike examples of healing, prophecy or miracles. But there are hints at tongues and various places where interpretations are given.

One narrative in which we see tongues used revolves around a king of Israel. In Isaiah chapter 38, King Hezekiah is sick and dying. The prophet of God has just told him to prepare for death. The king, in great travail, pleads with God to restore his life to him. Verse 3 says he wept before the Lord. Then the prophet hears from the Lord and King Hezekiah is given 15 more years. In the king's own words, he recounts, "like a swallow or a crane I chirp; I moan like a dove. My eyes are weary with looking upward" (Isaiah 38:14). His prayers were so deep in his heart, or his spirit, that the noises from his mouth resembled the tongues of birds more than man.

Such deep intercession resembled that of Hannah, who would be the mother of the great prophet Samuel. 1 Samuel 1:13 states, "Hannah was speaking in her heart; only her lips moved, and her voice was not heard. Therefore Eli took her to be a drunken woman. " But she was in deep prayer, not drunk. Likewise in deep prayer, Hezekiah chattered. Only the Lord knew what was in their hearts. 1 Corinthians 2:11 reminds us that the thoughts of a person are known in their spirit. And the thoughts of God are known by His Spirit. God knows all our thoughts and prayers, regardless of whether spoken aloud, in groans and mumbles, or prayed silently in our hearts.

In the book of Isaiah, the Lord makes a declaration that He Himself would use foreign languages to speak his messages. God chastised Ephraim, a tribe of Israel, because most of them had fallen away from the ways of God. Isaiah 28:11-12 reads, "For by people of **strange lips and with a foreign tongue** the Lord will speak to this people, to whom he has said, 'This is rest; give rest to the weary; and this is repose'; yet they would not hear." God can and will use other languages than a mother tongue to get His people's attention.

We will revisit this verse again, for the apostle Paul uses this verse to help the churches understand that God can speak to us through other languages. But first, let us continue examining other Old Testament examples of these two spiritual gifts.

Interpretations Abound

Although there are not many examples of the interpretation of spoken tongues, the general idea of interpretation is mentioned often in the Old Testament. Most interpretations are given for dreams and visions with their associated images. There are many clearly illustrated examples, from Joseph interpreting Pharaoh's dreams in Genesis 40 and 41 to Daniel interpreting dreams in the courts of Nebuchadnezzar and Darius throughout. Foreign soldiers correctly interpret dreams in the story of Gideon in Judges 7. And in Deuteronomy 13, the people of Israel were told to be wary of listening to prophets who use dreams to guide people away from the Lord.

But one of the most dramatic examples of an interpretation

is found in Daniel chapter 5. The interpretation was not of a dream, vision, or speech, but written words. The King of Babylon was conducting a huge party, and he desecrated many holy objects of the Lord. In the middle of the party, God pronounced a judgment against the king by sending a hand to write four words on a wall. None of the wise men knew the meaning or could interpret the words. A great fear fell upon the king and his assembled guests. Thus through the power of God, Daniel gives the interpretation:

> *"Then from his presence the hand was sent, and this writing was inscribed. And this is the writing that was inscribed: Mene, Mene, Tekel, and Parsin. This is the interpretation of the matter: Mene, God has numbered the days of your kingdom and brought it to an end; Tekel, you have been weighed in the balances and found wanting; Peres, your kingdom is divided and given to the Medes and Persians." Daniel 5:24-28*

The message was "Mene, Mene, Tekel, and Parsin." To the people present, these words were written in a foreign tongue. It was a mystery until interpreted. The king ordered an interpretation, not just a translation. Knowing that Mene means "a weight," Tekel means "to be weighed," and Parsin (or Upharsin, depending on the translation) means "divided" was not enough. The direct translation of these words does not solve the mystery of the meaning behind the handwriting on the wall. In verse 17, Daniel says, "I will read the writing to the king and make known to him the interpretation."

Interpretations, Not Translations

This is an important point to pick up at this juncture. Interpretation goes beyond mere translation. They are explanations. When God gave his prophets interpretations of dreams, visions, or written words, the meaning went beyond the translation of words, or proper descriptions of images. A deep understanding of meaning and purpose may be exposed by the Spirit of God.

In the Daniel example, God gave him divine understanding beyond words as he attached meaning to each word. Four written words became three statements which spoke God's judgment against the king and the nation of Babylon.

When I first started listening to people speak in tongues and give interpretations, I often wondered why such a short set of phrases (sometimes a very short phrase repeated many times) could generate such a long interpretation. I understood later that I was seeking a translation, whereas God, by His Holy Spirit, gave an expanded interpretation of the words spoken.

The spiritual gift described in 1 Corinthians 12 is not the gift of translation. It is not the ability to recreate word-for-word or phrase-for-phrase translations of one language into another language. Instead, the spiritual gift from the Holy Spirit is interpretation, which can include an expanded meaning beyond just the mere translation of words. This is important to remember as we move to a New Testament exploration of the gifts of tongues and interpretation of tongues.

Tongues in the New Testament

> *"But you will receive power when the Holy Spirit has come upon you, and you will be my witnesses in Jerusalem and in all Judea and Samaria, and to the end of the earth."* Acts 1:8

Numerous times our Lord promised the Holy Spirit to His disciples. Moments before Jesus left this world after His resurrection, He again promised the Holy Spirit to them. So the disciples continued to gather for prayer and worship waiting for the promise to be fulfilled.

Then on the day of Pentecost, ten days after Christ's ascension, the Holy Spirit fell on the disciples like tongues of fire. This was the day the Holy Spirit came and so did the gifts of the Holy Spirit. Though they were mentioned years later in Romans 12 and 1 Corinthians 12, the gifts of the Spirit appeared and began manifesting before Paul wrote about them. He wrote about them because the church was already interacting with the gifts and needed further instruction regarding them.

On the day of Pentecost, the Holy Spirit fell. That same day, Peter taught a profound sermon that caused more than 3000 people to start following Jesus. Peter again gave a sermon in chapter 3 of Acts, and more followed the Lord. Is this the natural preparation of a preacher or a gift of teaching bestowed on Peter by the Holy Spirit? It is most likely the latter, for we know he was not an educated man for he used simple everyday language (Acts 4:13, "they were uneducated, common men").

Similarly, when the Holy Spirit fell at Pentecost, the gift of tongues was activated in the first disciples. A clear description of what tongues looks like is found in Acts 2:

> *"And they were all filled with the Holy Spirit and began to speak in other tongues as the Spirit gave them utterance. Now there were dwelling in Jerusalem Jews, devout men from every nation under heaven. And at this sound the multitude came together, and they were bewildered, because each one was hearing them speak in his own language. And they were amazed and astonished, saying, 'Are not all these who are speaking Galileans? And how is it that we hear, each of us in his own native language? Parthians and Medes and Elamites and residents of Mesopotamia, Judea and Cappadocia, Pontus and Asia, Phrygia and Pamphylia, Egypt and the parts of Libya belonging to Cyrene, and visitors from Rome, both Jews and proselytes, Cretans and Arabians—we hear them telling in our own tongues the mighty works of God.'"* Acts 2:4–11

Verse 7 says the Galileans were speaking the languages of many other nations, some from very far away. The most common instance of tongues by the Spirit of God is being able to speak, for a time, in a foreign language that is known to another person.

Acts 10 and Acts 19 contain two more instances of when the Holy Spirit fell on groups of people and they started speaking in tongues. Acts 10 is when Peter first taught the gospel of Christ to the Gentiles in the house of Cornelius. And Acts 19 is when Paul comes across a group of believers that had only been baptized in water but not the Holy Spirit. The Acts 19 narrative is interesting because it also relates that the newly baptized disciples also started prophesying.

Interestingly, when Peter initially tries to explain the utterances in foreign language in Acts 2, he appeals to verses in Joel 2 which is about prophecy and not tongues. These verses speak of the pouring out of the Holy Spirit, but do not appear to have anything to do with tongues and languages:

> *"And in the last days it shall be, God declares, that I will pour out my Spirit on all flesh, and your sons and your daughters shall prophesy, and your young men shall see visions, and your old men shall dream dreams; even on my male servants and female servants in those days I will pour out my Spirit, and they shall prophesy." Joel 2:17-18*

Why did Peter appeal to this verse to support the gift of tongues being used? When the tongues of fire descended on the disciples at Pentecost, they were filled with the Holy Spirit and they started speaking in languages unknown to them that were nevertheless understood by the people of many nations attending the Pentecost feast. Peter makes the claim that these spoken tongues should be understood as fulfilling the promise of Joel 2. Why did the Holy Spirit prompt Peter to connect these verses from Joel to this outpouring of languages?

First, Peter is connecting Jesus' promise of the Holy Spirit to Jesus being given to us, where He said that God will pour out His Spirit. This is the main point Peter wanted to make: that what the people were seeing was the beginning of the fulfillment of God pouring out His Spirit upon people.

Secondly, all dreams, visions, and prophecies are ways for God to speak to us. Through interpretation of those dreams and visions, we can understand what God is doing in and around our lives. Similarly, God can speak directly to people through a foreign language, one not known by the speaker. This I believe is the second connection Peter was making. The people heard directly from God through spoken tongues in a way that was similar to a prophecy, dream, or vision. So again, it was a fulfillment of the outpouring of His Spirit prophesied in Joel 2.

As God poured out His Spirit so that old or young, male or female, all might know and communicate the truths of God, Peter saw strange tongues and their interpretation as just another way God's speaks. In a sense, the verse in Joel promised that God would speak to and through anyone when His Spirit is poured out. No disciple or apostle ever challenged Peter's idea that tongues indicate the presence of God's Spirit.

Tongues with Interpretation

In the Old Testament, strange tongues and interpretations are not mentioned together. But in the New Testament churches, the gift of tongues and the gift of interpretation are paired together in I Corinthian 12. They are meant to complement each other.

> *"To another various kinds of tongues, to another the interpretation of tongues. All these are empowered by one and the same Spirit, who apportions to each one individually as he wills."* 1 Corinthians 12:10-11

Generally, tongues and interpretation go together, as one without the other does not build up the body. The apostle Paul makes this point in 1 Corinthians 14:5, "Now I want you all to speak in tongues, but even more to prophesy. The one who prophesies is greater than **the one who speaks in tongues,**

unless someone interprets, so that the church may be built up." Without an understandable interpretation, a spoken tongue loses its effectiveness in a corporate setting. Paul gives an extended teaching on why an uninterpreted tongue is not fruitful.

> *"Therefore, one who speaks in a tongue should pray that he may interpret. For if I pray in a tongue, my spirit prays but my mind is unfruitful. What am I to do? I will pray with my spirit, but I will pray with my mind also; I will sing praise with my spirit, but I will sing with my mind also. Otherwise, if you give thanks with your spirit, how can anyone in the position of an outsider say "Amen" to your thanksgiving when he does not know what you are saying? For you may be giving thanks well enough, but the other person is not being built up. I thank God that I speak in tongues more than all of you. Nevertheless, in church I would rather speak five words with my mind in order to instruct others, than ten thousand words in a tongue."* 1 Corinthians 14:13-19

One goal of the church is to establish communities that are worshippers of God in both spirit and truth (John 4:24). In this passage, Paul affirms that it is important to build up your spirit, especially in prayer, so he speaks in tongues in his private life. But in the midst of a fellowship gathering, where the purpose is to build up each other, spiritual tongues do not have a place, unless they are interpreted. The reason being that Paul desired the minds of others to be built up with truth.

Paul affirms the need for both mind and spirit to be blessed and built up. He stresses that the mind of another person cannot be built up though tongues alone unless paired with an interpretation. That is why he opened the section with an exhortation to pray for interpretation (1 Corinthians 14:13).

Paul says to press in for prophecy because it does not depend on another gift to build up others as it presents itself in an intelligible language. Prophecy can bless all who hear the encouragement immediately, while an unknown tongue must be interpreted before it becomes an encouragement to others.

A tongue left uninterpreted is a mystery. Remember Daniel 5, the words "Mene, Mene, Tekel, and Parsin" were a mystery until interpreted. The spiritual gift of tongues without interpretation remains mysterious. It does not avail the heart or mind of others, nor can it encourage them. That is why Paul was unsatisfied with un-interpreted tongues. Without a clear message, there is no corporate edification.

A tongue without an interpretation highlights the one who speaks, but does not build up the common good. Remember, 1 Corinthians 12:7 says the goal is helping the common good. A highlighted "spiritual person" does not build up the congregation, only the person speaking. Thus in corporate settings, both large and small, there should not be a focus on tongues unless they are interpreted.

Additionally, the interpretation is for the community's safety. 1 Corinthians 14:16 says "how can anyone in the position of an outsider say "Amen" to your thanksgiving when he does not know what you are saying?" Part of the reason for an interpretation is that there can be things said in tongues that are not of God; interpretation is the only way for hearers to be able to say "amen" to what is good.

Always seek an interpretation for any tongue in a corporate setting. If none comes, then the assembled group can note that either the tongues were more human in origin than from the Holy Spirit or no one with the gift of interpretation was present. If a good interpretation does arise, then the community should be blessed, which is the best outcome.

Tongues Not Forbidden

We can clearly see the apostle Paul setting up two guardrails for all churches. First, all use of tongues in gatherings should always be interpreted. Second, tongues should not be forbidden or disapproved of. No spiritual gift should be off limits or scorned. These are the Scriptural guardrails for the practice of the gifts of tongues. These two guardrails keep us in the will of the Holy Spirit. We must never seek to shut down the gift of tongues (1 Corinthians 14:39, do not forbid tongues).

Quenching the Holy Spirit is a serious offense. In 1 Thessalonians 5, Paul ends the letter with a quick list of commands: "Do not quench the Spirit," (verse 19) followed by "Do not despise prophecies" (verse 20). When paired with the 1 Corinthians 14:39, the command to not forbid tongues, we have a clear set of rules to abide by.

Yet many churches and fellowships outright ban tongues and the interpretation of tongues in all gatherings. If you do not see the gift of tongues and interpretation ever used in your church, the spiritual health of the congregation should concern you. This is true if any of the spiritual gifts are missing.

Tongues and Interpretation in Action

For a few years, I was a part of a network of home groups that were earnestly pursuing all the spiritual gifts. They made room for any expression of the Holy Spirit and His gifts. In one of these meetings, I was profoundly touched by the Holy Spirit through an interpreted tongue. At the conclusion of acoustic worship, a young lady began to softly sing in an unknown language that sounded African in nature. Her voice rose in spontaneous song. The beautiful a cappella melody stretched for a few minutes, lifting our spirits and bringing most of us to tears. We were transfixed by the beauty of the expression of praise. She sounded as close to heavenly as we could imagine.

In wisdom, the leader of the group let the song linger a few moments, but he inquired of the group whether anyone felt there was an interpretation to the song. Two people offered interpretations focused on intercession for an African nation, which led us to a time of prayer. Our minds and hearts were able to gather in prayer because we pressed in for an interpretation of the song sung by the gift of tongues.

That evening we were both blessed in spirit, but we could also offer an "amen" to the intercession of the song once we knew the interpretation. We could agree with what was spoken, since we now had understanding. Such adventures and expressions await fellowships who allow space for the Holy Spirit to engage us across languages.

Do All Speak in Tongues?

It does need to be noted that some churches and fellowship groups believe that all disciples of Christ should speak in tongues. They use tongues as a mark of genuine faith in Christ or a marker of advanced spiritual maturity. I believe Scripture clearly communicates that teaching *all* should speak in tongues is *incorrect*, just as trying to forbid tongues it wrong. Let us consider Paul's writing on the matter.

> *"Are all apostles? Are all prophets? Are all teachers? Do all work miracles? Do all possess gifts of healing? Do all speak with tongues? Do all interpret?"* 1 Corinthians 12:39-40

The implied answer to all of these questions is "no," not everyone has each of these gifts. Not all gifts are manifested in every believer. Not all are apostles and not all speak in tongues. One could be full of the Holy Spirit and gifted as an apostle or prophet and not speak in tongues. We each have a ministry for the common good, equipped with some spiritual gifts as the Spirit of God determines. It is not Biblical to insist that a particular gift be manifested in each and every member of the church.

In summarizing the use of gifts, we can be guided with a few reminders. First, we do not forbid tongues. Second, hoping to edify all, we must seek interpretations for all spoken tongues. Third, we do not force anyone to speak in tongues. Tongues should never be used as a measure of authentic faith or discipleship.

Desire Tongues and Interpretation

But in the private setting, Paul highly encourages tongues, saying, "I thank God that I speak in tongues more than all of you" (1 Corinthians 14:18). This spiritual practice bolstered Paul's life so that he encouraged and challenged his readers to continue speaking in tongues at home. This teaching is sometimes neglected in many churches, though it is part of a rich spirit-filled life. Even as we desire to prophesy, we are to desire to speak in tongues.

We have not yet addressed the topic of a person having a prayer language (a particular tongue that they pray privately under the influence of the Holy Spirit for personal edification). Paul mentions prayerful utterances deeper than words (Romans 8:26) and speaking in tongues of angels (1 Corinthians 13:1). Such prayers and spirit utterances are not necessarily expressions of a spiritual gift. They are a part of spiritual disciplines which are beyond the scope of this book. Check out the Further Reading section at the end of this chapter to continue a deeper dive into the gift of tongues and interpretation of tongues.

Activate The Gifts

The gifts of tongues and interpretation has been controversial in many churches. In this chapter we have not sought to unveil or address all of those concerns. Our goal is to elevate these gifts into their proper place alongside the other gifts mentioned in 1 Corinthians 12 and provide reasonable context for their pursuit.

The church is built up by all the gifts of the Holy Spirit. Each fellowship group and every disciple should be in contact with people who express spiritually gifts, including tongues and interpretations. Any group that has never expressed or experienced tongues or the interpretation of tongues has room to pursue more of the Holy Spirit in their fellowship.

Let us join together in allowing the Holy Spirit to give and use these two gifts in our midst. Besides being a sign that the Holy Spirit is active in our midst (as Peter described tongues in Acts 2), tongues and interpretations are for the common good of every body of believers. Let us follow Paul's exhortation to earnestly pursue all the gifts and build up the body of Christ in all of the gifts of the Holy Spirit.

Discovering Your Gift

- Has God used you to interpret a human or heavenly language?
- At times do you feel speech in a tongue rising up in you?
- Have you felt you knew the meaning of something spoken in a language you do not know?

Faith in Action

- Consciously ask the Holy Spirit if you have been equipped with either the gift of tongues or interpretation.
- During a worship service, ask the Spirit of God if there is any spontaneous expression you could offer, be it in your native language or in another.
- Visit a church or fellowship group known for speaking in tongues. Not to join or be critical, but to experience other expressions of the Holy Spirit and the churches of Jesus.

Further Reading

- *Tongues,* Patricia King 2011
- *They Speak with Other Tongues*, Sherrill 2011 (reprinted)

CONCLUSION

My hope is to firmly establish each spiritual gift listed in 1 Corinthians 12 as a continuing right and privilege for all churches and fellowships of Jesus Christ. My desire is to awaken an interest, a new appetite, for the gifts of the Holy Spirit. God desires to equip the church so we can build each other up in love.

In Part 1 we established the need to pursue God both in truth filled and spiritual pursuits as worship unto Him. We also discussed how God moves in love and power. And how the power of the indwelling Holy Spirit is a promised aspect of what God has given every believer. Finally, we did a brief overview of a fundamental doctrine of 'laying on of hands" found in Hebrews 6:2, which is one means for releasing or stirring up spiritual gifts in each other.

Then in Part 2 of this book, we set a floor of expectation for each spiritual gift based on the Old Testament and the ministry of Jesus Christ. Then we furthered our study with an examination of how these gifts were administered through His disciples and then through the early churches. Together, these factors form a universal expectation that all the spiritual gifts should be known and active in our midst today.

Every Biblical fellowship and church should desire all the gifts of the Holy Spirit: from house church gatherings, to megachurch services, from cell church networks to local neighborhood fellowships. Every gathering of disciples will be strengthened more if all the gifts of the Holy Spirit are active in their midst.

Eagerly Pursue Spiritual Gifts

In this conclusion, I want to offer you encouragement to earnestly pursue the gifts of the Spirit, just as the early churches did. These gifts are not merely allowable to have, but God wants us to seek them out. The spiritual gifts are not meant to puff up ourselves but the Body of Christ needs continual strengthening and building up. As Paul noted in 1 Corinthians 14:12, "strive to excel in building up the church." We should all have a desire to build each other up. Beyond that desire, we should want our friends and family to be stronger in God. And leads to a pursuit of spiritual gifts so we can accomplish that desire.

Paul encourages the desire for spiritual gifts twice in the core chapters regarding spiritual gifts. First in 1 Corinthians 12:31, "earnestly desire the higher gifts" and again in 14:1, "pursue love, and earnestly desire the spiritual gifts." While we pursue loving each other, we should desire spiritual gifts. According to God's Word, it is acceptable to want more spiritual gifts, or a greater measure of a gift you are active in already.

Also, this pursuit of gifts and desire is not a one time endeavor. Just as we continually pursue loving our brothers and sisters in Christ, likewise we should continue to desire more spiritual gifts. It is not selfish or out of bounds to desire something God said we should desire. So stir up your pursuit of spiritual gifts, and help others fan into flames their spiritual gifts. Some practical ways to pursue spiritual gifts is to do a further Bible study of where the gift appears to be used, read a book about a particular spiritual gift, ask God for insight on how to use the gift, join a ministry where you can practice the gift, or use the gift in prayer or encouraging times in a community group. The Further Reading sections at the end of each chapter can be a starting point for investigating more deeply a particular gift.

Where To Go From Here

Picture this book less as a completed path and more as illuminating various trailheads that you can walk further in God's Kingdom. I made no attempt to fully characterize, explain, give detailed examples or walk you through pursuing any of these gifts in great detail. Each spiritual gift has the same great depth that God has. My hope was to create a bit of an appetite for each of these Holy Spirit distributed gifts and possibly stir up a desire for more and to spark a discussion among your community. Now you can go investigate more fully each gift as the Lord directs you.

Go back to each chapter and notice which gifts seem to resonate with the Spirit of God in you. Review the "Discover Your Gift" questions and linger on each, waiting for the Lord to confirm a gift or two in your spirit. Then, for the few gifts you want to investigate more, check out the "Further Reading" sections for entire books that are dedicated to that spiritual gift.

Next look for local or national conferences that are focused on the gift your are pursuing. Usually such conferences have prayer times where the laying on of hands for spiritual gift impartation is done. This is one way to step into the doctrine of laying on of hands, and receive from others what God wants you to carry.

Lastly, you can start where you are. Bring an awareness of spiritual gifts to your home fellowship, Bible study, or youth group. You do not need to try and teach anyone. Simply start using what God has given you. Let the love of God wrap your newly discovered spiritual gift and simply bless and serve others as an overflow of what the Holy Spirit is doing your life.

Be blessed knowing that God has given us every spiritual blessing. He showers us with grace, peace, hope, and love. Through the Holy Spirit, He blesses us with spiritual gifts that He has distributed to you and to all in your church. May we all continue to seek our Father, both in truth and in spirit, and to serve Him and each other through the gifts He has given.

> *"For this reason I remind you to fan into flame the gift of God, which is in you through the laying on of my hands"*
> *2 Timothy 1:6*

APPENDIX A: HOW GOD SPEAKS

God's ways, His thoughts, and His plans are infinitely higher than ours. When He wants to communicate His thoughts, feelings, ideas or plans to His children, He will use a variety of ways to speak to us. Every proper use of the spiritual gifts requires leading by God, and many gifts are highly dependent on real-time communication with God. Everything we hear from God must be tested against Scripture, which is our standard of truth. And God first and foremost speaks to us through His word.

We will provide a broad list of methods God can use to signal to us something He is doing or saying. This list is more targeted towards receiving words of wisdom, words of knowledge or discernment messages from the Lord; though prophecy and the other gifts will use these means too. These modes of receiving from the Lord also applies to your personal prayer life.

This reference list is gleaned from Scripture, but also represents the experience of various ministries like the Vineyard fellowship trainings, Global Awakening ministries and other trainings that I have had the pleasure of working through and teaching.

We are not going to cover all of the ways God can speak to us; we know He can get our attention through other people and situations or even answered prayer. In general, there are a variety of ways the Lord can speak to us, but this list is very helpful for receiving input from God.

Thoughts & Hearing

Light & Strong Impressions: an internal voice or what feels like spontaneous thoughts, words, or phrases, can be either faint or booming.

- "Immediately Jesus knew in his spirit that this was what they were thinking in their hearts" Mark 2:8. Other translations say He "perceived" their thoughts.
- This is really what might be called the still small voice of God in our hearts.

Audible Voice of God: people still sometimes hear the voice of God audibly or out loud

- Samuel heard the voice of God as a child (1 Samuel 3), Saul heard God from the blinding light in Acts 9:4, and Moses heard God on numerous occasions. I have a personal friend who, when at a very low point in his life, before he met Christ, asked out loud if any one cared about him, and he heard audible voice behind him say, "I care." He very soon after gave his life to the Lord.

Seeing & Images

Pictures: a still image or a sequence of images that flash through your head. Almost like a photo or a painting popping into your mind.

- Jeremiah is given a picture by God and also hears God's voice at the same time.

- "And the word of the Lord came to me, saying, "Jeremiah, what do you see?" And I said, "I see an almond branch." Then the Lord said to me, "You have seen well, for I am watching over my word to perform it." Jeremiah 1:11-12 and a similar account in Jeremiah 24:1-5

Inner Visions: internal movies playing in your mind. Some say "light" if they are short or end if they are not focused on, and "strong" if they are longer or can resume when prayerfully seeking the Lord for more.

- The "strong" variety are what many of the Old Testament prophets, like Ezekiel, Jeremiah, or Daniel describe: "I, Daniel, had a vision, after the one that had already appeared to me" Daniel 8:1. Genesis 15:1 "the word of the LORD came unto Abram in a vision" and again, Daniel 2:19a "Then the mystery was revealed to Daniel in a vision of the night."

Open Vision: a vision that is so strong, the participant cannot discern the vision from the real world.

- Daniel 8:2-3 says "And I saw in the vision, and I was at the Ulai canal. I raised my eyes and saw, and behold, a ram standing on the bank of the canal." The vision was so engrossing, he thought he was in another place.
- And again, in Ezekiel, he similarly felt as though he went to Jerusalem even as he sat with the elders in chapter 8.

Seeing the Invisible World Visibly: the Lord may open our eyes to see what is happening in the spiritual world

- "Then Elisha prayed and said, "O LORD, please open his eyes that he may see." So the LORD opened the eyes of the young man, and he saw, and behold, the mountain was full of horses and chariots of fire all around Elisha." II Kings 6:17
- Balaam's donkey sees an angel: Numbers 22:23 "And the donkey saw the angel of the Lord standing in the road, with a drawn sword in his hand." "Then the Lord opened the eyes of Balaam, and he saw the angel of the Lord standing in the way, with his drawn sword in his hand. And he bowed down and fell on his face." Numbers 22:31

Trances: characterized by being awake but not fully conscious or responsive

- Peter fell into a trance – Acts 10:9-11 "Peter went up on the roof to pray. And he became hungry and wanted something to eat, but while they were preparing it, he fell into a trance. He saw heaven open and something like a large sheet being let down to earth by its four corners."
- Paul Acts 22:17-18 "When I had returned to Jerusalem and was praying in the temple, I fell into a trance and saw him saying to me, 'Make haste and get out of Jerusalem quickly, because they will not accept your testimony about me.'"

Dreams: divine dreams scattered throughout the Bible, there are so many that we will not try to list them all.

- Symbolic Dreams: Joseph, both as a dreamer and as an interpreter gives many examples of symbolic dreams that were from God (Genesis 37:5-10 and Genesis 40-41). Much of the book of Daniel is also concerned with frightening symbolic dreams from God. Even unbelievers can have dreams from God: Pharaoh, the King of Babylon, and even foreign warriors (Judges 7:13-15).

Literal Dreams: such dreams can be taken more or less at face value, like Paul's dream of a Macedonian man asking him to come there (Acts 16:9)

Angelic/Messengers in dreams: Jacob had a dream of angels ascending a ladder (Genesis 28:12). Joseph, the father of Jesus, had a dream of angels speaking to him (Matthew 1:20, Matthew 2:12-13 & Matthew 2:19)

Emotions & Physically

Physical Sensations or Emotions: feel a wind that is not there, a pressure of a hand, tingling ear, trembling, quaking, heat or happy/sad feeling

- "And he said, 'Go out and stand on the mount before the Lord.' And behold, the Lord passed by, and a great and strong wind tore the mountains and broke in pieces the rocks before the Lord, but the Lord was not in the wind. And after the wind an earthquake, but the Lord was not in the earthquake." I Kings 19:11
- "And when they had prayed, the place in which they were gathered together was shaken, and they were all filled with the Holy Spirit and continued to speak the word of God with boldness." Acts 4:31
- "But this is the one to whom I will look: he who is humble

and contrite in spirit and trembles at my word." Isaiah 66:2b

Visitations

Angelic Visitation: Abraham, Lot, Mary, Joseph, Zechariah, Daniel and others all had encounters with angels

- "When I, Daniel, had seen the vision, I sought to understand it. And behold, there stood before me one having the appearance of a man. And I heard a man's voice between the banks of the Ulai, and it called, 'Gabriel, make this man understand the vision.' So he came near where I stood. And when he came, I was frightened and fell on my face." Daniel 8:15-17
- "The two angels came to Sodom in the evening, and Lot was sitting in the gate of Sodom. When Lot saw them, he rose to meet them and bowed himself with his face to the earth." Genesis 19:1
- "The revelation of Jesus Christ, which God gave him to show to his servants the things that must soon take place. He made it known by sending his angel to his servant John." Revelation 1:1
- Hebrews 13:2 reminds us that at times we may be unaware of angel visitation, "Do not neglect to show hospitality to strangers, for thereby some have entertained angels unawares."

Visitation of Jesus: Samson's parents (Judges 13), fiery furnace (Daniel 3), Abraham and Sarah (Genesis 18)

- "And the donkey said to Balaam, 'Am I not your donkey, on which you have ridden all your life long to this day? Is it my habit to treat you this way?' And he said, 'No.' Then the Lord opened the eyes of Balaam, and he saw the angel of the Lord standing in the way, with his drawn sword in his hand. And he bowed down and fell on his face." Numbers 22: 30-31
- "And the angel of the Lord came again a second time and touched him and said, 'Arise and eat, for the journey is too great for you.'" I Kings 19:7
- Paul had such an encounter in Acts 9:3-7: "suddenly a light from heaven shone around him. And falling to the ground, he heard a voice saying to him, 'Saul, Saul, why are you persecuting me?' And he said, 'Who are you, Lord?' And he said, 'I am Jesus, whom you are persecuting...' The men who were traveling with him stood speechless, hearing the voice but seeing no one."

Other

Caught up in the Spirit

- (Paul) "I know a man in Christ who fourteen years ago was caught up to the third heaven—whether in the body or out of the body I do not know, God knows. And I know that this man was caught up into paradise—whether in the body or out of the body I do not know, God knows— and he heard things that cannot be told, which man may not utter." II Corinthians 12:2-4
- John on Patmos: "After this I looked, and behold, a door standing open in heaven! And the first voice, which I had

heard speaking to me like a trumpet, said, 'Come up here, and I will show you what must take place after this.' At once I was in the Spirit, and behold, a throne stood in heaven, with one seated on the throne." Revelation 4:1-2

APPENDIX B: CONCISE LIST OF SPIRITUAL GIFTS

Gifts of the Holy Spirit

> *"For to one is given through the Spirit the utterance of* **wisdom***, and to another the utterance of* **knowledge** *according to the same Spirit, to another* **faith** *by the same Spirit, to another gifts of* **healing** *by the one Spirit, to another the working of* **miracles***, to another* **prophecy***, to another the ability to* **distinguish between spirits***, to another various kinds of* **tongues***, to another the interpretation of* **tongues***... And God has appointed in the church first* **apostles***, second* **prophets***, third* **teachers***, then* **miracles***, then gifts of* **healing***,* **helping***,* **administrating***, and various kinds of* **tongues***." I Corinthians 12:8-10,28 ESV*

WISDOM: 1 Cor. 12:8. Greek: sophia - wisdom, application of knowledge

Spiritual intuition or supernatural revelation pertaining to applying Godly truth to a current situation, resolving a problem, or giving practical instruction. A sense of being guided by the Spirit in circumstances in order to take appropriate actions.

WORD OF KNOWLEDGE: 1 Cor. 12:8. Greek: gnosis - knowledge, knowing

Supernatural revelation of information; to know something you have no way of knowing except by revelation of the Holy Spirit. These facts are testable. To know a testable current or historic fact that you never learned and know without any human aid, attributed only to Divine help.

FAITH: 1 Cor. 12:8-10. Greek: pistis - faith, assurance, belief

Spiritual surge of confidence which rises within a person in a particular situation of need or challenge and gives an extraordinary certainty, trust, and assurance that God is about to act. To have unshakable conviction and be firmly persuaded of God's power in a circumstance and to fight off unbelief until it is resolved.

HEALINGS: 1 Cor. 12:9,28,30. Greek: iama - from root ioamai - to heal, cure, or make whole

To be a conduit of supernatural healing, meaning without human aid. To make one whole includes physical, emotional, mental, or spiritual healing. To command a healing in Jesus name and see it happen. To do through the Spirit, as Jesus did when He healed the sick.

MIRACLES: 1 Cor. 12:10,28. Greek: dynamis - miracle, mighty work, power, force

A mighty supernatural work enabled by God that is beyond that which is natural and performs mighty deeds. To exercise authority over the natural laws, sin, infirmity, and forces that cause hindrances to the Kingdom purposes. Miracles can validate the message of God that comes with the worked miracle (I Thes 1:5, I Cor 4:20)

PROPHECY: Rom. 12:6; 1 Cor. 12:10; Eph. 4:11. Greek: propheteia comes from prophetes (prophet): 'pro'=fore; 'phemi'=to say or declare

"The one who prophesies speaks... upbuilding and encouragement and consolation." I Cor 14:3. Speaking an inspired message of God, not just from intellect, in the known shared language. Inspired divine anointed declaration: message, vision statement, calling, gifting, or future oriented events. These messages can be heard from God, spiritually seen in a vision or dream, or flow as the person speaks.

DISCERNMENT, DISTINGUISHING BETWEEN SPIRITS: 1 Cor. 12:10. Greek: diakrisis - distinguish, discern, decide, judge ('dia'=through/with, "krino"= distinguish/separate)

A supernatural knowing of whether the behavior, activity, or teaching is from God, Satan, human error, or human power. To clearly distinguish not by intellectual means or observation, truth from error or pure from sinful motives. Can imply the possession of spiritual senses of vision, hearing, or emotions to reveal the spiritual world of the enemy and his forces (demons), as well as, God and His messengers (angels). To rightly determine if actions, attitudes, works, teachings, or beings are of the camp of God or Satan. Discernment is not characterized by suspicion or accusation.

TONGUES: 1 Cor 12:10, 14:27-28. Greek: glossa - language, dialect, speech, tongue/bodily organ

To speak in a language not previously learned by inspiration of the Holy Spirit. These languages can be in current use on earth, come from ancient culture, or a language never used by any earthly cultural group considered an "unknown" tongue. (Acts 2:4; 10:44-48; 19:1-7; I Cor.12:10,28-31; 13:1-3; 14:2,4-22,26-31).

INTERPRETATION OF TONGUES: I Cor 12:10, 14:27-28. Greek: hermeneia - interpretation or translation of something spoken

Supernatural ability to know the content of words spoken in another tongue without having learned that language. It functions, not as an operation of the human mind, but of the Spirit. To translate the message or general meaning of what someone has spoken in tongues; this does not have to be a word for word translation.

APOSTLE: Eph. 4:11; 1 Cor. 12:28. Greek: apostolos - apostle, messenger, sent one ('apo'=from 'stello'=send; one sent forth)

To be a representative of God, to be sent out and carry a message of God and His word from a position of leadership (Acts 6:2). Providing leadership and vision over church bodies and maintaining authority over spiritual matters pertaining to the church. To have vision for and establish new Kingdom works and advance the Church into new frontiers.

TEACHING: Rom. 12:7; 1 Cor. 12:28; Eph. 4:11. Greek: didasko - teach, taught, instruct, impart instruction

To be able to study, apply, and explain the truths of God, usually from Biblical text, with an inspired or supernatural ability. This is in contrast to the prophet who is seen to be speaking from the mouth of God, who's message does not require learning or study. The teaching presentation can be through various forms of speaking, writing, creative art, song, play, or Bible studies (ie. Bible study teacher, children's ministry teacher, Bible study writer, etc...). The teaching may be for an individual or crowds.

SERVICE, MINISTRY, HELPS: Rom. 12:7, 1 Cor. 12:28. Greek: diakonia - servant, deacon, attendant, minister, serves food; Helps (antilēmpsis) to aid or help

To minister or serve with supernatural love and care to those in need like a deacon, and thus free the leaders to other duties. To assist, help, serve, or support others directly in their ministry. To help and serve the body of Christ in practical actions. This may be supporting the Church by cleaning, serving food, caring for the sick, organizing, making flyers, setting up chairs, running cameras or sound equipment, etc.

ADMINISTRATION: 1 Cor. 12:28. Greek: kybernesis - steer, guide, government, director

Spiritual ability to steer the body toward the accomplishment of God-given goals by planning, organizing, governing, and supervising others. Running ministries toward the goals set by the leadership team and given by God. Keen understanding of the Kingdom goals and supernatural implementation to reach those goals. Under the power of the Holy Spirit, organizing service teams, Church event planning, making calendars, keeping schedules, communicating events or information, etc.

Gifts Given by Grace

> *"Having gifts that differ according to the grace given to us, let us use them: if **prophecy**, in proportion to our faith; if **service**, in our serving; the one who **teaches**, in his teaching; the one who **exhorts**, in his exhortation; the one who **contributes**, in generosity; the one who*

> ***leads**, with zeal; the one who does acts of **mercy**, with cheerfulness." Romans 12:6-8*

EXHORTATION: Rom. 12:8. Greek: paraklesis - calling to one's side, exhort, console, comfort

Literally means, "calling to someone" to encourage him. Encouragement, comfort, consolation, or reminding (Acts 4:36; Heb. 10:25). This can be spoken encouragement, writing notes, etc.

GIVING, CONTRIBUTING: Rom. 12:8. Greek: metadidomi - give, share, impart

Giving in a spirit of generosity to share what material resources you have with liberality and cheerfulness without thought of return through the power of the Holy Spirit. This includes being led by the Spirit where and when to give. This gift should be exercised liberally, without ostentation, control, or boasting (II Cor. 1:12; 8:2; 9:11,13). It can mean to provide resources to those who do not have them.

LEADERSHIP: Rom. 12:8. Greek: proistemi - to be over, to stand before, superintend, preside

To be "placed at the front in some activity". To stand before the people in such a way as to attend supernaturally to the direction of the group. To lead with such care and diligence so as to motivate others to get involved in the accomplishment of these goals. To embrace model action, care, supervision, and direction by leading of the Holy Spirit.

MERCY: Rom. 12:8. Greek: eleeo - mercy, compassion, pity

Identifying and attending to those suffering whether physically, mentally, or emotionally with supernatural grace.To be sensitive toward those who are suffering and can include feeling genuine sympathy with their misery while remaining cheerful. Speaking words of compassion and caring with deeds of love, a listening ear, or just being present to help alleviate their distress.

Equippers as Gifts

> *"And he gave the **apostles**, the **prophets**, the **evangelists**, the **shepherds** and **teachers**, to equip the saints for the work of ministry, for building up the body of Christ" Ephesians 4:11-12*

The role of these various equippers is not covered here, just their giftings.

EVANGELISM: Eph. 4:11. Greek: euaggelistes - preacher of gospel or messenger of good news ('eu'=well, 'angelos'=message)

To be a messenger of the good news of the Gospel of Christ to people in darkness through spiritual empowerment. To preach and to witness to bring unbelievers unto salvation.

SHEPHERDING (PASTORING): Eph. 4:11. Greek: poimen - shepherd, pastor, herdsmand, manager, director

To disciple, to be responsible for spiritually caring for, protecting, guiding, and feeding a group of believers entrusted to one's care through the power of the Spirit. To care, protect, lead, nurture the people in ones care. This can include a small group leader, children's Sunday school teacher, spiritual mentoring or discipling, recovery group, etc.

Other Possible Gifts

> *"Show **hospitality** to one another without grumbling. As each has received a gift, use it to serve one another, as good stewards of God's varied grace: whoever **speaks**, as one who speaks oracles of God; whoever **serves**, as one who serves by the strength that God supplies" I Peter 4:9-11*

HOSPITALITY: 1 Pet. 4:9,10. Greek: philoxenos - hospitable, fond of guests and strangers ('philos'=fond/love, 'xenos'=stranger)

To warmly welcome people, even strangers, into one's home or church as a means of serving those in need through the power of the Spirit. It was manifested in lavish care to believers and workers who came to visit, to worship, labor and form part of the body of Christ. This can include hosting a small group, welcoming people at church, serving church lunches, hosting missionaries in your home, taking in foster or college students, etc.

MISSIONARY - *not specifically mentioned in the Bible*

This is usually either an evangelistic or an apostolic person who is taking the Gospel to a new people group or starting new Kingdom works. This can include facing cross-cultural dynamics, remote areas, and unknown situations.

INTERCESSION - *not specifically mentioned in the Bible*

Praying for others, usually for longer periods of time, with a firm resolution that your prayers will be heard. A supernatural deep desire, burden, and joy to pray for others: unbelievers, fellow believers, the needy or sick, those in sin, nations, ministries, etc. The desire to pray may be stirred by another gift like prophecy, words of knowledge, faith, or mercy.

About the Author

Greg Holsclaw seeks to stir up passion for God's heart and to empower people in all walks of life. As a pastor, author and technology manager, Greg has a unique perspective to encourage believers, founded on his rich Biblical tradition and his ability to help other partner with the Holy Spirit.

He is the founder of Revival Valley, an equipping ministry touching hearts in Silicon Valley where he also pastors a small fellowship and has been married to his wonderful wife Tracy since 2002.

You can connect with me on:

http://www.revivalvalley.com/empowered

https://www.facebook.com/gregholsclaw.page

https://www.instagram.com/holsclawgreg

Subscribe to my newsletter:

http://eepurl.com/gDqxRr

Made in the USA
Las Vegas, NV
22 September 2023